THE ART OF MAKING SH!T UP

NORM LAVIOLETTE

USING THE PRINCIPLES OF IMPROV

THE ART OF MAKING SH!T UP

TO BECOME AN UNSTOPPABLE POWERHOUSE

WILEY

Published by John Wiley & Sons, Inc., Hoboken, New Jersey.
Published simultaneously in Canada.

For general information on our other products and services or for technical support, please contact our Customer Care Department within the United States at (800) 762-2974, outside the United States at (317) 572-3993 or fax (317) 572-4002.

Wiley publishes in a variety of print and electronic formats and by print-on-demand. Some material included with standard print versions of this book may not be included in e-books or in print-on-demand. If this book refers to media such as a CD or DVD that is not included in the version you purchased, you may download this material at http://booksupport.wiley.com. For more information about Wiley products, visit www.wiley.com.

Library of Congress Cataloging-in-Publication Data is available:

ISBN 9781119558217 (Hardcover)
ISBN 9781119558309 (ePDF)
ISBN 9781119558316 (ePub)

Cover Design: PAUL MCCARTHY
Cover Image: © GETTY IMAGES | MASSIMILIANO ALESSANDRO / EYEEM

Printed in the United States of America

V10009064_032919

This book is dedicated to my incredible wife, Kelly, and my amazingly talented and beautiful daughters, Chloe and Lucy. Thank you for letting a grown man play make-believe for all of these years.

CONTENTS

CONTENTS

INTRODUCTION

Listen, we all make shit up to a degree. Call it testing, iterating, innovation, ideation, hypothesis. It all boils down to the same thing: We are making shit up as we go and figuring it out from there. At its worst, it can make us feel like frauds. The fear that someone will call us on our bullshit and we will be exposed for the uneducated, untalented charlatans we are can stop us in our tracks, holding our desire and ability to do something new and different and meaningful hostage.

At its best, it is the truest form of intellectual freedom. Creating something from nothing, free of judgment or even the expectation of results. Originality and innovation blossoms from deep in the recesses of the mind, not because some people have the magical creative gene, but because they have overcome the fear of judgment of others and themselves. As a poet once said, "To make shit up one first has to not give a shit" (no poet ever said such a thing).

So the question is, how do we use this thing that we all do for fun and profit? How do we take this much-maligned concept, often correlated with the idea of being unprepared and undisciplined and turn the concept on its head? After all, if nobody ever made shit up, nothing would ever exist.

Let's all come to an agreement here, shall we? It will make this whole thing easier as we continue. Making shit up is a skill. It may be a skill that you do not currently recognize or appreciate, like being able to whistle through your nose or snake a clogged drain. These are things that can be learned. And once learned, the skill level can be improved upon by repetition of action. The more one does a thing, the better one will inevitably get at the thing.

Repetition leads to familiarity. Familiarity leads to comfort with the task. Comfort with the task allows one to take more chances and find better ways to do the task. Finding better ways to do the task leads to the development of skill. Skill is important, because before we have art, we must have a level of skill. Skill is the platform that art is built upon.

Making shit up is also an art. I mean, if I didn't believe that, then the title and premise of this whole book would be even more suspect than it already is. Doing something artfully requires more than just the rudimentary functions of executing a task. It requires a certain amount of thought and intent. Skill needs to be exhibited in some way, consciously or not, but there for the eyes to see or the brain to experience. And anything can be artfully done. One can just as easily artfully plate an elegant dish as one can artfully pass gas.

The actual task does not define if something is artful. The same is true for making shit up, or if you are already tired of reading the word "shit" so often, having a creation mindset. Developing a creation mindset, where you can start to see possibilities everywhere, is a learned skill. It can be learned by anyone on a very practical level. It ain't magic and it ain't a divine gift to the specially anointed. No different from snaking a drain, the basic skills of how you develop the creation mindset just needs to be taught. Once the skill is learned, it can be artfully deployed towards any subject of your choosing.

Developing a creative mindset allows us to consider new possibilities or solutions to problems, be they mundane or great, practical or existential. Having a creative mindset allows us to exist in an environment where that mythical and elusive spark finds us, as opposed to us constantly searching for inspiration and meaning.

These are heady thoughts of the philosophical nature of making shit up. Exactly the kinds of thoughts that I find on the one hand inspirational and on the other hand entirely useless if not followed up with practical "how to do it" instructions. You can tell me I should "have" a creation mindset just as easily as you can tell me I must "have" a Kobe beef cheeseburger. Sure, sounds great. But where the hell do I go to get that Kobe burger?

In the chapters that follow, we will explore not only the whys of making shit up but the hows as well. Let's be honest with ourselves; since we are already bullshitting our way through a good majority of our lives, we might as well embrace that fact and learn to use it for good.

Chapter 1

I Am Who I Say I Am

I'm an improvisational comedian. This is what most defines me as to who I am today. What I do and how I think comes from the fact that I've spent tens of thousands of hours making shit up in front of people.

For some ungodly reason, I thought it was a good idea to get on stage in front of people and try to make them laugh using whatever happened to be going on in my mind at that time. Call it hubris, narcissism, or a pathological need for people to think I was something special, I decided that yes, I had something funny to say, and yes, you should be subjected to what that is.

Disregard the fact that I more often than not had nothing funny to say, and there was absolutely no one clamoring for my genius ... well, that's not entirely true, my mother loved everything I did, no matter what. Biggest fan in the world, especially considering there really wasn't much to be a fan of, in my formative years.

On a practical level, how did I come to the idea that not only did I want to get up in front of strangers and make something out of nothing, but that I actually could get up in front of strangers (and many times sympathetic and supportive friends) and play make-believe?

Let's start with the basics: I came from a funny family. Mom was hilarious, Dad was crazy and funny, and my sisters all knew how to get a laugh. We were surrounded by oddball aunts and uncles (my mom comes from a family of 19). You needed to be able to hold your own to keep the focus in the midst of a lot of loud, little French Canadians. The most prized skill of all was being funny. If you were funny, you had a seat at the table. You could be a blowhard uncle or a swearing and slightly racist aunt or an accomplished foreign diplomat. If you were funny, you were in.

My first memories of watching comedy are of sitting on the couch after school watching Abbott and Costello in black and white on Channel 27 in Grafton, a small mill town in Central Massachusetts. I loved the physical comedy, as well as the word play: Bud Abbott smacking Lou Costello for screwing something up, the constant misunderstandings, overemoting, insults ... I loved it all.

There weren't many rules in my family when I was a kid. Come to think of it, I can't think of one single "official" rule I was required to follow. It was never a problem if I wanted to stay up late and watch *SNL* when I was 8, or Monty Python movies when I was 12. I watched Cheech and Chong, *Airplane, Blazing Saddles,* all from the comfort of the horrible floral-print couch in the parlor (that's what my people call the living room), all while my parents, aunts, and uncles played hearts, argued and swore and laughed under a constant white-blue cloud of cigarette smoke in the kitchen.

This is also where I gained my affection for curse words. My mom was a world-class cusser bundled into a 4-foot, 10-inch French Canadian frame. The woman was loud and swore like a trucker. And before anyone gets all up in arms about my stereotyping truckers, I know whereof I speak, as my dad was in fact a trucker.

My mom could give both George Carlin and Richard Pryor (and for the younger set, Amy Schumer and Brian Callan) a run for their filthy money. And I would give the nod to mom because she could do in two languages. So if you are a sensitive soul or in any way offended by the title of this book or the other swear words judiciously sprinkled throughout, please blame Cecile. I promise you, she would definitely not give a shit about what you think.

And TV shows. Oh, how I loved those '70s and '80s sitcoms. Happy Days and the Fonz jumping cars and doing crazy Greek dances. Watching *All in the Family* with my mom, with Archie Bunker as a racist foil, the physical comedy of John Ridder in *Three's Company*; *The Jeffersons, Soap, Mork and Mindy* and *Cheers.* I consumed it all, all the various types of comedy and laughter pouring into my feeble child's brain, scarring it for the rest of my life.

I especially loved the HBO Comedy specials. Listening to Richard Prior majestically unleash "motherfucker" after "motherfucker" was like listening to Pavarotti hitting the highest of high notes. George Carlin, Eddie Murphy, Steve Martin, Robin Williams. I was mesmorized.

How could these people be so outrageously funny, holding audiences captive and forcing laughter to come pouring out uncontrollably? It was like a magic trick, getting people to respond the way you wanted them to, whether they wanted to or not. The absolute fearlessness with which they stood on stage speaking their truths with an "If you don't like me, I don't give an "F"" attitude. It wasn't rock bands or guitar players or even actors or movie stars for me, it was these guys. They were my rock stars and I watched them so much that I could recite their entire routines along with the TV.

After you've spent your weekend watching SNL, with Gilda Radner's Rosanne Rosannadana derailing Jane Curtin on Weekend Update, or Robin Williams spiraling into the ether on improvisational tangents at Carnegie Hall, showing up on Monday for fourth grade feels a little underwhelming. It became my mission to make everyone laugh. Girls, boys, nerds, jocks, quiet kids, smart kids, dumb kids, freaks, stoners, geeks, and goobers – I was a populist when it came to obstructing my classmates early educational pursuits.

I would employ jokes, stupid comments, props, slapstick (falling back in the chair was a favorite because it was funny, but also gained sympathy from the teacher)—whatever elicited a reaction was okay by me. The one-on-one stuff was great, but when I could get the whole class to laugh, including the teacher, well, that was the ultimate feeling of control. Twenty-eight fourth-graders and an adult laughing because of something I did or said? It delivered a powerful jolt to my young brain that said *Hey, it feels damn good when people laugh at what I do or say*.

Many kids use humor as a defensive mechanism when they are young, either to keep people from picking on them or as a way to make friends. That really wasn't my motivation. I didn't struggle with either of those issues. For me it was the sheer pleasure of getting a laugh.

That laugh felt better to me than anything else in the world. So I spent a good part of my days trying to get that feeling.

Of course, at some point my teachers had to get on with what they were being paid to do, so I spent a lot of time either in the back of the room by myself (which I didn't mind), in the hall (which I didn't mind), at the principle's office (which I didn't mind), or with my desk moved all the way to the front of the room pushed flush against the teacher's desk (which I hated).

Yet even when I got "in trouble," I always had the sense that I wasn't *really* in trouble. It always seemed to me there was a smile lurking just behind the stern look and serious words that the teachers would have to use to set me straight. Basically, I didn't believe them. They thought I was funny, too, and I knew it.

Being funny became my thing, from elementary school all the way through college. That, and motorcycle racing. I bet you didn't see that coming. I come from a motorcycle family. The first time I rode a minibike by myself, I was three years old. My grandfather, Big Al (Fat Pepe to me), owned Al's Cycle Shop in Palmer, Massachusetts, along with my Grammy, Shirley. My dad, "Big Norm" (I'm still referred to as "Little Norm" by much of the family), raced motorcycles from when he was a little kid to age 65. My uncles Bobby and Albert and Aunt Jeanie all raced as well.

My dad or mom would run beside me as I rode a minibike, my legs so short that I couldn't touch the ground. At some point I rode faster and faster until I just rode away from my dad. He recalled, "I didn't know if you knew how to turn or use the brakes, but there was nothing I could do, so I just hoped for the best." Clearly a very different parenting style from today's helicopter parents.

I raced motorcycles from age 7 until early college. People thought my parents were crazy for letting me race. And yet for me and my family, it was normal – more than normal, it was second nature. When I raced it felt natural and safe, as well as thrilling and a little "F" you'y, too.

Looking back on it now, I have a much clearer view of how it affected me. As a kid racing motorcycles, it instilled in me the belief that I could do much, much more than the regular world thought was possible, or even prudent or sane. Teachers and parents speak in platitudes, like "You can do anything!" and then freak out whenever a kid deviates ever so slightly from what the collective culture deems "appropriate" or "safe."

Risk is a part of life. Facing risk and overcoming it is one of the keys to achieving something great. Did my parents put me on those minibikes recklessly and without thought to my safety? Of course not. I had to wear every piece of safety gear imaginable. I had to learn and understand the machine. I had to fall down at slow speeds, take some bumps, and understand that a crash at high speed was going to be far more painful, so I better know what I was doing.

I also learned that those bumps and bruises didn't last forever, and that I could get back up and ride again. And as time went along, I noticed a change in people. They were impressed that such a small kid could master something seemingly so risky. They took a greater interest in who I was. They wanted to hear more about what I did. And I started to realize something: I could do more than what most people thought was possible and others would want to hear about it.

Also, I learned about failure. Every race there was exactly one winner. It was hard to finish in first place. I had 100 times more second-place trophies than first-place ones. More often than not, someone was beating you. Yet I learned that I could compete, get better, and have fun. After a while I started beating some of the sons-a-bitches who had beaten me for years. Lesson: Have fun and actually try to win – do those two things and you will get much, much better.

High school was more of the same, except throw in football, a girl-friend named Nina, and the somewhat reckless behavior common to boys and girls in the 80s. 'Nuff said.

While I enjoyed school socially, I was mostly bored, lazy, and undis-ciplined. Nothing much else had changed: I'd make my classmates and my teachers laugh, the teacher would eventually have to kick me out, and I spent a lot of time in room 10, the in-school suspension room. I didn't really mind. It was usually quite fun to hang out with the skids, freaks, druggies, and losers. I got along with them as well as anybody else. And I learned that if you didn't really care about cer-tain things, like getting into trouble, the authorities lost their power over you. I wasn't a dumb kid, but I was no academic super star by any stretch of the imagination, so I got a lot of "progress reports" that were better known as "warnings."

Problem was, I would never bring them home and would just have one of my female friends sign my parent's name, so there was no one signature to compare to. By the time I was a junior or senior, I stopped playing the charade all together. I got a "warning" notice from my math teacher, Mrs. Langas (hated math but loved her). I said: "Look, you and I both know I'm not going to bring this home and show it to my parents. Even if I did they wouldn't care. So I can either just give this back to you or get it signed by someone else. What would like me to do?" She took it back. She was awesome.

Also, I learned how to cheat. Today I refer to it as "academic life hacking," simply finding efficient shortcuts to achieve my academic goals. I may not have wanted to do the work, but I sure as hell wasn't going to fail everything, stay back, or get kicked off the football team, so I had to do something. I got really good at academic subterfuge. And not your garden-variety crib notes or copying or scribbling answers on the hand. I had all that in my repertoire, sure, but I was more sophisticated than that. The great thing about being funny, charismatic, and popular (and also an unfair advantage over the kids who are not) is that you aren't as suspect as those who are perceived as "undesirables". When you can equally chat up a teacher as well as a classmate, you don't draw as much attention when you are the only one in a classroom searching through a teacher's desk for the grade book. (Now the advantage goes to the technology kids and computer hackers, so I guess I hit high school at just the right time.) I changed a lot of minuses to pluses, Ds to Bs, and 60s to 80s. I managed to get my hands on an entire Spanish midterm exam, take it to the town library, copy the whole thing, and sneak it back to the teacher's desk without her ever knowing it was gone.

Am I proud of all of this? The mature and self-aware answer is "No, I am not. I now know that I should have worked harder and applied myself to my studies." That would also be bullshit.

I am kind of proud that I could figure out a way to beat the system, working my way around the things that didn't interest me. And I felt that if no one particularly was hurt, then what was the harm? The harm was that for a long time I didn't have the discipline to complete things, to push through tasks that were unpleasant or not exactly what I wanted to do. The result was to make things harder on myself, because if I had done it right the first time, everything would have been much easier.

Fast-forward to 20 years later. A career in comedy; improv comedy no less. Starting up several companies. There is a clear and obvious pattern in my life. What I learned racing motorcycles stuck with me. I could face risk. I could face failure on the stage (and believe me, fail I did, and sometime still do). I could face failure in business (I have had a couple of doozies). I could master things I didn't know. Things could be done that others said were not probable or prudent or safe. Bumps and bruises, to the ego as well as the bank account, could be overcome if I just forced my ass back on the bike/stage/business world.

Some people think risk is to be avoided, or at least mitigated. I think risk is thrilling. It's the electrical current that galvanizes our souls. Take a risk. It doesn't have to be skydiving or starting your own company. Maybe it's making that call that you have been too nervous to make. Maybe it's following that idea that you have had but have always been told that it is too crazy. Maybe it's telling someone "I love you." Whatever it is, go take a risk. It's scary. If we are going to make some shit up, we are going to have to take some risks. And when the risks pay off, it feels pretty damn good.

Chapter 2

Listening to Understand

Thinking is hard. There are so many obstacles that we put in our own way when it comes to thinking; we don't have enough time or talent or creativity. We are constantly distracted by social media or children or pets. Life, man.

Thinking under pressure is even more difficult. With a time constraint put on the process, thinking can feel downright impossible. We can experience tunnel vision, a real experience brought on by not breathing, which limits oxygen and blood to the brain, which in turn limits that same blood and oxygen going to the eyes. (Yes, yes, smarter people will explain this more scientifically but basically this is what's happening.)

Self-judgment, criticism, lack of confidence and self-esteem all contribute to the ability or lack thereof to think quickly or creatively. Overthinking can lead to paralysis and indecision. Information over-load can give us too many options, so much that we can't pick one idea and move on it. I call this the Cheesecake Factory effect. There are so many damned options on that menu that I always end up getting the same thing (jambalaya, in case you are wondering). Thinking, at its worst, is often focused on the negative aspects of what is going on or what might go wrong.

Thinking is also a deeply internal activity. By its nature it is introspective, focusing on what is on the inside and cutting out the external noise. For so many of us shutting off those outside distractions is a huge challenge. Focusing inward is not something most of us get to do on a regular basis, be it because of our jobs, families, lifestyles, or the culture that we are brought up in.

The modern world is basically designed to make thinking and focusing incredibly hard. So much so that we even now have drugs specifically designed to help us focus and pay attention. If that isn't a sign that artificial intelligence will soon be taking over running our lives, then I don't know what is.

Listening, on the other hand, is something that we are forced to do every day. Listening is the main way most of us receive information, both simple and complex. It is a function and a skill that we begin developing at birth. From the first soothing sounds a parent makes to comfort a newborn baby, we hear things and begin to process that information and try to make some kind of sense of it.

Listening is done passively all the time. In the car listening to radio, watching TV, in class or in a meeting, or listening to your boring-ass friend tell another one of their pointless stories about what they did last weekend. Passive listening takes no real effort. Much like breathing, it just happens. We don't sit down on the couch and consciously say to ourselves "Okay, I now have to listen to *Game of Thrones* as I also watch it."

How much information we retain is a different matter, but the act of passive listening is mostly subconscious and does not require much thinking or effort to do so. Anybody can listen, and in fact almost everybody in the entire world already does.

People ask me all the time what is the most critical skill for a successful improv comedian to develop. Most think that it is the ability to be funny or to come up with ideas out of nowhere. Some people think it is a gift that comes naturally, the ol' "you either got it or you don't" syndrome. Many assume that you need to be extroverted and have incredible charisma or a larger-than-life personality. None of this is correct.

The single most important thing that makes an improv actor successful on stage is his or her ability to listen. To the other actors. To the audience. The concentration point is always on the other person, hearing what they are saying and reacting to that.

We are trained in improv to focus our attention on the other person. To listen to what they are saying and respond to what we have heard, not what we think. This is a very different style of listening from passive listening. Improv actors and comedians are trained to actively listen. The improv actor focuses on what is being said and tries to truly understand what they are hearing. Actor A then responds to the dialogue that was just spoken by actor B. Instead of thinking of something to say or trying to invent some kind of funny response, all actor A has to do is respond to what actor B just said. Actor A's concentration is solely on the sentence just spoken by actor B. In that sentence there will be plenty of details to respond to. Let's look at an example. We will set the scene in a train station:

Bob: *Looks like the train is running late again.*
Helen: *Unbelievable! This is going to make me late for my job
              interview.*
Bob: *What company are you interviewing with?*
Helen: *Livingroom.com. It is a new startup that is essentially Airbnb
              for your living room. If you don't have friends or family to
              watch your favorite TV shows with, you can schedule time
              with someone else's friends and family.*
Bob: *You are not going to believe this, but I am the CEO of
              Livingroom.com.*

Let's take a look at this scene. Aside from it being a fairly poorly written improv scene (it played a lot better live on stage), this is a good example of how listening to your scene partner will give you as an actor all the information you need to respond. With the first line of dialogue Bob states, "Looks like the train is running late again." Helen only has to process this information and respond, "Unbelievable!" That is all. Helen did not have to invent any crazy scenario or pull some amazing concept out of the ether. She simply listened to Bob and responded to what she heard.

Helen's next line of dialogue "This is going to make me late for my job interview" adds context as to why she is waiting for the train and how that train being late will affect her. Bob only needs to respond to what Helen just said. All he has to do is find one thing to reference in Helen's response.

In this example Bob focuses on the fact that Helen is late for a "job interview." This allows Bob to respond in a very simple and natural way with the question "What company are you interviewing with?" No wild invention or clever responses needed. Helen in turn now only needs to answer Bob's question. In this instance my answer (I'm playing both the role of Bob and Helen) is somewhat more elaborate for comedic effect. It would work just as well if Helen had said:

A bank
A library
Dunkin' Donuts
Anything the hell she wanted to say

Bob then reacts to what he hears and defines a relationship to what Helen has just said, in this case by being the CEO of the company she is going to interview with.

By listening to each other and responding to what is being said, Bob and Helen have removed "overthinking" from the communication process. This was not passive listening, though. With each sentence Bob and Helen picked out one detail to understand and drive their response.

I know, you're probably saying to yourself "That's it? Obviously this is what has to happen. It is what people do all the time." I beg to differ. Let me show you how that scene or scenes like it have often played out. We will get the exact same scenario of a train station:

Bob: *Looks like the train is late again.*
Helen: *Here comes the C train, right on time.*
Bob: *It is so annoying, the T never runs on time.*
Helen: *Here it is. Let's get on and head to Fenway.*

Beyond the astoundingly bad dialogue, we see two people who have heard the initial idea of "train station" but are not listening to each other at all. Each person is working on and sticking to their own agenda. With each separate line of dialogue, both Bob and Helen have to keep inventing ideas.

Eventually a couple of things will happen. First, Bob and Helen will most likely run out of new ideas. Second, it is pretty obvious that they are not on the same page and the conversation will end up being confusing and frustrating for both of them.

I have witnessed conversations like this both on stage and off thousands of times. People talking around a subject but not actually to each other. When we talk "at" each other, as opposed to "with" to each other, it puts us in our own head and forces us to have to think. Instead of responding and creating a give-and-take of ideas, we often get caught up in a loop where the individual keeps restating the same idea or versions of that idea. Nothing original is being created, or if it is, it is either one-sided or competing against another idea.

This kind of conversation often leads the feelings of frustration. That sense of "You aren't listening to me" or "You are not hearing what I'm saying." This creates a disconnect between the two people trying to communicate with each other, which can lead people to shut down communication altogether. The "screw it, why bother" attitude takes over, and the exchange of ideas comes to a screeching halt.

Another version of the "Not Listening" trap is "Predictive Listening" or "Thinking Ahead." We have all been in conversations in which we have thought to ourselves "I've heard that one thousand times before." We hear something familiar, maybe even something that we *have* heard a thousand times before, and instinctually we tune out, because we know what we are about to hear. This leads us as the listener to come up with a response well before the person speaking to us has finished their entire thought. Typically we begin to tune out and adopt the attitude of "Wrap it up, dude, I know what you're going to say and here is my brilliant response."

The problem here is that what may have started out as something we have heard one thousand times before has a very different ending. By not actively listening all the way through, we miss critical information and in fact respond to our own preconceived thoughts and ideas.

Here is an actual situation that happened to one of our clients at Improv Asylum, discussed during a corporate training session:

One of our salespeople was trying to close a large sale to a new client. When presented with the total cost of the service we were providing (a software product), the client responded "That is more expensive then what we were hoping for. What we are really concerned about is if you can deliver what we need on time, within the short time frame that we need it."

Well, the salesperson stopped listening when they heard "… more expensive than we were hoping for …" They assumed the price was the main factor in determining if the sale was going to be made. The salesperson started thinking about their response without ever hearing the end of the client's concern.

The salesperson replied: "You know what, as a new client we can offer you a discount of 15 percent off the price."

The client responded: "That's great, we are still worried about you being able to deliver the product on time we need."

The salesperson responded: "Oh, we can definitely get this expedited for you so you can meet your deadline."

Had the salesperson listened all the way through, they would have understood that the client's concern or pain point wasn't necessarily price but rather time of delivery. The salesperson may have unnecessarily given away 15 percent of the sales price. And if you think about it, the salesperson could have used the fact that the company could get the client what they needed within the time requirements, thereby justifying the cost.

That is a perfect example of not listening all the way through and assuming what is going to be said. We all do it all the time and it often leads to missing new or critical information. Missing that kind of information is death in an improv scene. The actors won't be on the same page and the audience will be confused. The actors will have to work that much harder to come to an agreement and be able to move the scene forward.

While it is all just make-believe for us on the stage, missing this kind of information in a business environment has all kinds of potential consequences, from affecting sales to enabling a culture of colleagues that don't listen to each other, which leads to low morale and a lack of innovation. In personal relationships, it often leads to that feeling of "You're not listening to me!" That is never a great place to be in our relationships.

So what can we do to get better at active listening? While there are all kinds of high-level theories around listening and how you can be better at it, I like to keep it simple because I am a simple man. Like anything, the more you practice, the better you will get. A technique I use is the "immediate playback" technique.

Here is how it works: When you are listening to someone speak, play the game of repeating in your head what the other person is saying as they are saying it, word for word (you can do this out loud, but you might come across as slightly insane).

This is a great exercise to do when you're forced to sit in excruciatingly boring meetings. Before I became the person who was boring everybody in meetings, I would try to stay engaged by repeating sentence by sentence or word by word what the speaker was saying. Doing this forced me to stay focused on what exactly was being said and would stop my mind, at least for a little while, from wandering to other topics.

Another technique is to make and hold eye contact with the speaker. Eye contact is probably one of the most, if not the most, powerful ways that humans can communicate with each other. (With animals as well. Have you ever noticed how disconcerting it is when an animal locks eyes and stares at you? There is something primordial about looking into another being's eyes.) When two people have eye contact, it's nearly impossible to think about anything other than what the person is communicating to you in that moment.

Obviously, as the listener, you do not have full control of whether eye contact is being maintained if you are in a setting where you are just receiving information. But if you are in a conversation you can initiate the eye contact that will allow you to focus on what is being said.

One thing that makes eye contact so powerful is that if you initiate the contact, it is very difficult for the other person to break it. Therefore you are not only increasing your own attentiveness but you are forcing the attentiveness of the other person.

Eye contact is a common trick in public speaking and live performance. If you keep making and holding eye contact with the various members of the audience, they have to listen to you in the moment, and also are cognizant that you may be coming back to them. That is why you will often hear the advice, "Don't just talk to the crowd, talk to individuals in the crowd."

The benefits of concentrated and active listening are the same for groups and organizations as they are for individuals. When a team employs Active Listening, the benefits are exponentially increased. The individuals in the group feel like they are being heard and therefore have a higher level of engagement and "buy-in" to the culture or organization.

We are all big boys and girls and understand that not every decision is going to be exactly what we want it to be. For most people, as long as they feel like they have truly been heard and have had a voice in the discussion, they can accept the decision more easily when it does not go their way.

By focusing on other people when they speak and actively listening to what it is they're saying, our minds are freed from thinking, which allows us the ability to respond. "Thinking fast" is more a function of being able to respond to what you hear than of thinking of something to say. This in turn allows us to understand and process more information, which invariably leads us to make often-unexpected connections. And making unexpected connections is just another way of saying "making shit up."

Chapter 3

Building Off of Other People's Ideas

So you are listening. You're making strong eye contact, and you are playing back the words that are being spoken in your head. You are nodding positively to outwardly show that you are engaged and interested in everything that is being said to you. Swell.

The upside to this skill is that maybe you are gaining and retaining a better understanding of what you are hearing. The downside is that now people think you are a great listener or "sounding board" and your newfound empathy has people wanting to bare their souls to you. Sorry about that.

Whether you want to become a more sympathetic confidant or just someone who wants to do more/try more/be more, so much of it starts with listening and building off of other peoples' ideas. What does "building off of other peoples ideas" mean, exactly? Does it mean stealing other people's ideas? Does it mean not being original? Does it mean subjugating your own creativity and individualism to constantly support other people's efforts?

Hells no! What it means is that you are learning to find inspiration from other things outside your own brain. Other peoples' ideas are the fundamental building blocks of improv, as a skill and art form.

As we have already discussed, the ability to listen actively and try to as best as possible understand what is being said is the first step in being able to improvise on stage. Yet if the only thing we do is listen, then we become a sponge, absorbing information but never really doing anything with it. If we are going to make shit up, we have to do shit with the knowledge and information we gain from listening so damn hard. That is where the "building" part comes into play. The building part is where we allow ourselves to find inspiration and add our own creativity and imagination to the initial idea or concept.

In any kind of team setting the ability to listen and build off of each others' ideas allows the group to quickly access many different concepts. Because each team member is a stakeholder in the chain of ideas, each member can lay claim to a certain amount of ownership of the final creation. Not only that, but individuals do not need to feel they have to be a superstar creative who has to come up with ground-breaking ideas all the time. If the culture is one where the group builds off of other ideas and makes incremental contributions to concepts already in existence, then even those team members that may naturally be more reserved can participate in the ideation and innovation phases without feeling the pressure of being "creative."

In the world of improv we are trained to listen and positively accept our scene partner's "offers" or ideas. What this means as a basic practice is that instead of always having to think of something new, we can listen to somebody else's idea and associate and be inspired by what they say and whatever we hear.

An improv actor knows that the other actors are going to do the same thing, so each has the confidence to add on and build off of the initial concept. The goal is to take the thinking out of it and focus on listening, making a connection, and responding.

In the initial ideation phase, as long as you're responding to what was said by the other actor, it doesn't really matter what you say. As long as your response is inspired in some way by what your scene partner just said, then there is no wrong answer. Let's take a look at a basic Word Association exercise. I'll start with a word, any word; for example:

Pineapple
Chunk
Goonies
Movies

Popcorn
Butter
Ball
Masquerade
Intrigue
Assassination

All I did in this exercise is to associate directly from one idea to get to another. The initial concept is "pineapple." By associating from one word to the next, I quickly build to the end concept, which is "assassination." While this is a very basic ideation exercise, it essentially illustrates the fundamentals of improv: listening and building off of other ideas. The concept of pineapple doesn't have any direct connection with the concept of assassination. But by listening and building off of each previous idea we can quickly arrive at seemingly unconnected yet wholly original ideas.

I now can go back and evaluate which ideas I want to work with. Maybe the idea of an "assassination at a masquerade ball" is the first scene in a new novel. Or maybe it is the concept of holding a "Masquerade Butter Ball" charity fundraising event sponsored by the dairy industry. Whatever, we now have more options to consider simply because we listened and built off of earlier concepts.

This word association exercise is one you can do by yourself or with a team. The great thing about doing an exercise like this with a group is that once the idea is finalized, each member of team feels like they made a contribution to the end product. It may not be exactly what any one person originally thought it was going to be, but instead is a completely original idea with input from multiple members.

Another exercise we teach at Improv Asylum is something we call "Electric Company." Named after the trippy children's educational TV show from the 1970s and 1980s, this exercise takes the concept of listening and building even further. In the first exercise that we did above, we used fully formed words. In Electric Company we respond to less fully formed ideas. This is how it works:

Person number 1 says half a word. Maybe the word he or she has in mind is "police." Instead of saying "police," the actor just says "po-."

Person number 2 listens to the first half of the word, in this case "po-," and comes up with an ending to the word. The next syllable might be "-et," creating the word "poet." Maybe the actor comes up with "-lenta" or "-go stick" or anything else that he is inspired to say.

Then both actors speak in turn to say the new word: "poet."

Person 1:   *"Po-"*
Person 2:   *"-et"*
Person 1 and 2 together: *"Poet"*

They both say the new idea together to reinforce the new concept. The game, as it were, is not necessarily to guess the original word that person number 1 was thinking, but rather to listen to the initial idea and be inspired to add on whatever ending comes to person number 2's mind. Instead of having competing ideas you have ideas that are owned equally by both people. Again, you can always go back and pick the one that you like best, but now you have more options, and no matter which one you choose both parties will feel like they had some kind of input, which leads to a greater sense of ownership of the final idea.

This may all sound great and inclusive and *kumbaya*-ish, but as AC/DC said "I tell you folks, it's harder than it looks" (*A Long Way To the Top If You Wanna Rock 'n' Roll/TNT*). For one thing, we are generally not raised to make other people's ideas better. Pretty much our entire lives we are taught that there is great value in being an original thinker. We are told to stand up and fight for our ideas. In the end my idea wins, your idea loses, I get the job, raise, promotion, blue ribbon, and all the accolades while you wallow in self-loathing and a crippling jealousy of my unique talents. I mean, come on, why the hell would I want to make your idea better if that is going to put you ahead of me? And in a zero sum game where each individual is out for themselves, it doesn't make a lick of sense.

Ah, but here is the thing. In improv we are trained to create together. We are taught, not unlike sports or the military that the greater goal is for the team to succeed and not any one individual. With improv we create as an ensemble and try as best we can to stick to the ethos of accepting each other's ideas while also letting our own ideas get changed or modified.

Letting our own ideas be changed or modified is the second thing, and I think it's the biggest challenge. Fear of change is intrinsic to our basic humanity. Most of us love our own ideas. They are our babies. We incubate them and nurse them and feed them and only expose them to this harsh and terrible world when we are ready. They are a manifestation of what is inside us; our creativity, talents, and worldview. Once we allow our precious ideas to be brought forth for all to see and judge, the last thing we want to happen is to have them changed.

Imagine if you had a child, created under very delicate circumstances and nurtured and guarded with the utmost of care for nine months. In the midst of your insecure thoughts about whether or not you are good enough to actually take care of a baby, she arrives for all to see. You are a proud parent and after much deliberation you arrive at the perfect name for this one-of-a-kind inspiration.

You name her Chloe. A group of friends and loved ones gather around to admire this astounding new creation of yours. They look at baby Chloe, admiring her rosy complexion and her thick black baby hair and immediately begin to suggest improvements.

"I love her hair, but imagine how cute she would look if it were red."

"And the name Chloe, I mean, I like it, but what if we made it more modern sounding?"

"Ooo, oh yeah, how about instead of Chloe we call her Joey, but Joey spelled Joei so as not to impose any kind of meaning that may be attached to an old-fashioned name like Chloe."

You would be saying, "Hold the F on! That's my baby! You can't just go and change how she looks and what her name is. I created her. She is mine. You have no right to alter this perfect creation."

It is the same thing with ideas. They are our mind babies. We cherish them and guard them and so often feel that they are perfect just the way they are. This is almost never the case and it doesn't matter if you are creating on your own or with a group. There is nothing that is created perfect and fully formed right out of the gate. It doesn't matter if it's a joke or concept or product, everything needs to be looked at, edited, and iterated. This is the process we use to go from basic or starter concepts to bigger and more expansive thoughts. It is also the process that requires the individual to let go of his or her ego, at least for a little while.

Letting your idea get changed even a little bit requires a certain amount of bravery and confidence. Bravery in the fact that you don't know if the changes to your initial idea is going to be successful, and confidence in the fact that ultimately you have many more ideas that you can come up with, and that any one particular idea is not the be-all and end-all of what you have to offer the team, company, or universe.

Each of these skills – listening and building off of other people's ideas as well as letting your own ideas be modified – becomes stronger with practice. The more you exercise your brain, the more your brain will become used to this process. What you will eventually find is that there is inspiration all around you. Initially it may come from listening to other people.

As you become more accustomed to associating off of the information that is given, you will start to see connections or possibilities in all kinds of unexpected places. Those unexpected connections are what lead to innovation.

Instead of racking your brain trying to come up with the next brilliant concept or idea, you will find it is more fun and far easier to open your mind and observe and listen to what is going on around you. You then build upon that initial stimulus to come up with new and exciting possibilities.

Full disclosure, I now own the concept of the Masquerade Butter Ball. Land O'Lakes, give me a call if you want to blow this concept out. This ball would be off the hook!

Chapter 4

From Spark to Flame

I don't believe that ideas hit you like a lightning bolt, pouring out of you fully formed like some sort of mystical vision or 3-D printer. Even when it seems like it does, the reality is that your subconscious has been influenced every step of the way since you popped into this f'd up world.

Whatever you are thinking or creating at that moment has been molded and shaped by millions of different stimuli, seen and unseen. What that means is that creativity is inherent in all of us, even if you work in insurance. Since nothing comes out fully formed; the trick is not to capture this blazing vision in its entirety but rather to identify the spark.

The spark. The lightbulb. The aha moment. The quickening. The fingersnap, the head slap, the "By George, I think I've got it" moment. This is what we are looking for. This is what our mental radar is constantly sweeping back and forth in search of, trying to identify those blips of inspiration splayed across our neural pathways, and somehow bring them to life as something concrete.

Identifying those moments when we can say to ourselves, "You know what, that is not a half-bad idea" is the starting point for making shit up. And really it can be the easiest and most fun part of the whole shebang. Completed and executed ideas? Scary and hard. Short bursts of inspiration with no real outcome? Easy and fun!

So in my perpetual quest to make my life as easy and as fun as I possibly can, I spend a large part of my creative process looking for those moments.

So how does one go about finding the spark? Or does it find you? Honestly, I have no idea. What I can tell you is that there are a few commonalities in my life that have consistently led to new and interesting ideas and opportunities. Let's take a look at them.

CURIOSITY

Curiosity has been one of the main reasons that I have been fortunate enough to live such an interesting and creative life. Allowing ourselves to be curious opens our mind to receiving new information. Diving into the how or why or where of something will immediately return dividends of new knowledge. Allowing yourself to pursue interests for no reason other than the fact that something intrigues you or delights you or confuses you is reason enough to go down the rabbit hole of whatever subject you are exploring.

When you allow your curiosity to drive you to explore new concepts, you create new data points in your brain. You may consciously retain some of those data points but you will invariably dump a whole bunch of them, consciously or not. It doesn't matter. What you are trying to do is fill your "subconscious thought well" with thoughts and feelings and snippets of ideas that your brain can reference on its own.

When we speak about ideas coming out of nowhere, that is never true. They come out of that subconscious "thought well" that you have been filling up throughout your life. The more curious you are, the more and different experiences or pieces of information you pour into the well, making them available at some later date.

We will only draw from the well what we put into it, so if we just sit around on our asses doing basically the same old thing and thinking the same old thoughts again and again, we can expect to get the same results.

DO SHIT

I am a lousy spectator. I have a hard time being interested in anything that I can't do or at least try. That tactile, tangible experience helps me to be able to thoroughly process information. If something captures my curiosity, invariably I want to try it.

I have always found that by doing the things that I am curious about, I have been able to get a deeper understanding of whatever subject I am exploring. Moving from a passive role to an active role activates the entirety of your body and ingrains whatever it is that you are doing in a far deeper way.

You like flowers? Go out and actually pick them. Like watching rugby and don't know how to play? Buy a rugby ball and play catch with somebody. Interested in military history? Go walk, or better yet ride a horse, on a battlefield.

Clearly your ability to do something will be dictated to a degree by what you are physically able to do. The point is that when you actually go out and physically experience whatever you are most interested in, it becomes a part of you in a way that it can never be if you are just watching.

The unexpected benefit that comes from doing things is the circumstances that surround any activity. It is on the edges and in the fringes that the magic and unseen connections start to happen. By choosing to go "do shit," you put into motion all the things around that activity.

If you decide you want to take up bicycling it will eventually lead you to a bicycle shop, where you will meet people with your same interests. Meeting people with similar interests means you will be connecting with a certain number of those people who have more knowledge and information about bicycling that they will share with you.

From that information you will learn about events centered around bicycling. This may lead to you wanting to participate in a charity ride. By joining that ride, you may find a whole new cause that you want to support. That cause may become one of the most important things in your life and bring great value and joy to yourself and those you help.

And all this occurs because you became curious about bicycling after watching a few hours of the Tour de France and decided to explore it.

Far-fetched? Hardly. The fact that you set something in motion can't help but have a ripple effect, because nothing happens in a vacuum. Each decision made has many different side effects that ultimately open up more doors and windows to be explored. So the trick isn't to try to open up many different doors and windows, but to make one decision to do something, anything, and then pay attention to what happens off to the sides. There on the side streets are where you will find the fascinating and unexpected connections.

OBSERVE

I consider observing to be very different from spectating. Observing is a purposeful activity where you are consciously focusing on what you are seeing, hearing, or feeling. When we are observing an event, we are actively taking in information and processing it for later use. Spectating is a more passive form of receiving information, more conducive to enjoyment or entertainment. One is not necessarily better than the other, they just facilitate different functions.

When we observe an activity we tend to see both the micro and the macro of the event. If we go to a football game and observe what is going on, we see the players on the field, of course, but we also see the thousands of people in the stadium, the flashing signage, the TV cameras, where security and police are positioned, the cheerleaders and the beer vendors and the drunk dudes two sections away fighting with each other. We take in the entire scene in the macro, yet also pick out specific details in the micro.

When spectating, on the other hand, we tend to focus on a specific thing: the players on the field, the ball, and the score of the game. We tend not to notice or be overly caught up in all the other things that are going on around us because our attention is directed toward the activities that are entertaining us. This specific focus is what allows us to lose ourselves in the moment, be it getting caught up in the excitement of the football game or lost in a particularly moving piece of art. The focus on what is happening in front of you becomes so specific that you don't notice, nor do you need to, the environment around you. You are caught up in the moment, which in and of itself can be immensely pleasurable.

Observing is important to the process of making shit up because you are again taking in various different data points. You are consciously and actively receiving new information. When you start at the macro level and then slowly begin to focus the lens on the micro details, you start building that subconscious database where bits of information can swim around and potentially knock into each other.

While observing, you aren't necessarily trying to make connections, but in receiving this new information it allows potentially unrelated concepts to collide. The idea of beer vendors and policemen might seem unrelated. Yet if we allow those concepts to collide, maybe something new happens.

Maybe the idea of having undercover officers walk the stadium dressed as vendors is a way to increase security. Or maybe the beer vendors have a direct line to the security staff so they can alert them if trouble is brewing. The security staff can then make their presence felt prior to things getting out of hand, and hopefully diffuse the situation before it blows up into something bigger.

By consciously observing what is going on around us we have yet another way to capture the raw material that will be turned into ideas. Observing doesn't take a ton of effort and it takes no money. It is another simple thing we can control and is incredibly helpful in stocking the larder of the mind.

FAN THE SPARK

So we are following our curiosity, which is leading us to do shit, and we are observing what is happening around us, which is leading to sparks.

Now what? In very simple terms, sparks will die out if you don't capture them and fan them into something bigger. I do not claim to have any special ability to identify good ideas or have any singular talent that allows me to do things others can't. The one ability that I do have that so many people I encounter do not, is the ability to recognize a spark when I see it

Every day, people come across sparks of inspiration. An idea comes to mind and a small flash of excitement courses through them as they say to themselves "Hey, that's a pretty good idea." And then they never do a damn thing and the spark dies out like a sparkler on the Fourth of July. All you are left with is a flimsy piece of wire and second-degree burns.

The ability to jump on the spark is the single most important thing for making shit up, in my not-so-humble opinion. Look, every asshole has ideas, it's the assholes who do anything with the ideas who can make a difference in their lives.

The ability to identify and then act upon the initial surge of inspiration is what puts all things in motion. So the question is, how do we identify the spark, and then how do we have the courage to grab it and fan it into a fire?

For me the key to identifying a spark is when I get unabashedly excited about something. When I have a positive emotional reaction to an idea, that usually means there is something there to take a look at. I try not to judge or feel embarrassed by this emotional reaction. If for some reason I am now superexcited about looking for mushrooms in the woods, I try to embrace the excitement for what it is, a flash of interest that makes me feel good. If it makes me feel good or is intellectually stimulating I'll continue exploring the idea.

Once it no longer feels good or stops being intellectually stimulating, I let the idea fade away. I do this over and over again, allowing myself to become excited about something, and exploring it a little bit, and then letting it die. Some people will say that this is a lack of focus or a needless exertion of creative energies. I say these people are idiots. I say this for a couple of reasons.

First, exploring what brings pleasure or intellectual stimulation is usually a worthwhile pursuit. If something makes me feel good (and isn't unhealthy and doesn't hurt anyone else), why not pursue it? If it is intellectually stimulating, meaning it makes me think and grow on a personal level, then what would be the reason not to explore the idea?

Second, in following the little inspirations even a short way down the path, I'm practicing my ability to create momentum for potential ideas. What others consider lack of focus, I consider it to be a practical way of finding inspiration.

One hundred sparks will die out for every one that flickers to life. That is perfectly okay and acceptable. I'm sure there are more talented people than I who have a higher spark-into-flame rate. For me it is all about volume. I firmly believe that if I allow enough sparks to start, eventually one will catch. Or, I will freeze to death, alone and unremembered except by those closest to me. Either way, I will have enjoyed myself.

If one hundred sparks die out for every one that ignites into a small and fragile flame, how does one know which ideas to pursue and which ones to give up on? While this of course will be different for each individual, in my case what I end up identifying as ideas worth pursuing are the ones that show themselves in a couple of different ways. The first and the easiest way is when the excitement just doesn't die. When a concept grabs a hold of me, digs in, keeps me so excited that it just seems obvious that I need to jump on it and see where it goes, I follow it as far and as enthusiastically as I can.

This most recently happened to me in New York City. I learned that a former improv theater in Manhattan was vacant and available. Following my ethos of "curiosity" and "doing shit," I immediately scheduled a visit with some key members of my team. Upon seeing the theater and the opportunity it presented, I was immediately struck by the excitement of what Improv Asylum might be able to do in this space. It took me no more than a few minutes to decide to pursue the idea of creating Improv Asylum New York in this theater.

There were many times along the way that the concept could have fallen apart. Yet I didn't worry about any of that. I concentrated on following the idea to its next logical step, in this case contacting the landlord and seeing if they would be willing to rent the theater to my company. Each decision led to the next, to the point where we officially launched Improv Asylum New York in November 2018.

The second way is the "zombie" way. This is when an idea just keeps coming back again and again. These ideas just keep clawing their way back to life, no matter how many times I bury them or put them on the backburner or send them to bed. If the concept keeps coming back into my consciousness no matter how far I move away from it, then I decide there must be something that is worth exploring.

When an idea keeps resurfacing, I begin to believe that my subconscious is telling me that there is something here, so pay attention. For me, this was China. For years I had been boring my staff and anyone who would listen to me about my belief that the biggest frontier for improv is in China. A culture with a deep history of creativity and an immense population hungering to once again move to the forefront of originality and innovation, China seemed to me to be the perfect place to bring the concepts and ideas of improvisation and the theories of modern collaborative creation. My staff would humor me, listening to my wild speculations about bringing improv to China and waiting for my current passion to subside.

Year after year the idea of developing a program in Chinese gnawed at the back of my head. So much so, that I pitched the idea year after year to one of our colleagues at Harvard Business School, where we run an annual program. Knowing that HBS had a campus in Shanghai, I would offer the idea of developing our corporate improv training techniques in Chinese. Each year I would get the polite "That sounds interesting" response and be sent on my merry way.

Until one year when the organizer of their global leadership group said "Do you think you can really put something together like this in Chinese?" This lead to Improv Asylum developing an entire program in Mandarin with some fantastic Chinese improvisers who are now our partners in bringing our philosophies on improv, creativity, and culture to growing companies and universities in China.

Unlike the New York theater, which came about incredibly fast, our Chinese program was the result of an idea that just wouldn't die. It kept coming back to me and reigniting my interest to such a degree that I had keep pushing and exploring the idea, even when most everybody else thought that I was a bit nuts.

Like everything I have talked about up to this point, the ability to identify the spark and then grab it and fan it can be practiced. Start small. When something excites you, immediately explore the concept. This might mean just researching it online to start.

It doesn't matter how strange or arcane others may think it is. If it excites you, then immediately pursue it just a little way down the path. Keep doing this with many different ideas. Have fun seeing where and how far your explorations go. Most interests will die a natural death, and that is okay. What you really are doing is strengthening that muscle that allows you to make connections and let things seemingly spontaneously combust.

Allow yourself to be unselfconsciously curious, get out and do shit, and observe the world around you. If you do this, you will start to experience the feeling of inspiration finding *you* instead of you finding it.

I want to be clear here that this is just one way of creating and finding inspiration. There are one million ways to create, and if somebody claims that there is one singular way or right way to find inspiration, pack your bags and head for the hills.

What I am describing is a process that works very well for me and may also for you. You most certainly can create in a methodical, disciplined, and well-thought-out way. In fact it ends up requiring quite a bit of discipline to keep exploring ideas when you categorically know that most will go nowhere. Yet the ability to identify and fan the spark is, for me, the cornerstone of making shit up and getting shit done.

Chapter 5

The Fear of Looking Stupid

The fear of looking stupid is often one of the biggest reasons we don't go after the things we really want. There are so many barriers, actual and tangible – money, time, health – to exploring ideas or trying new activities that we would like to pursue. These are obstacles that are real and that we may not have complete control over. But looking stupid? That is all on us.

I'm sure psychologists and anthropologists can trace back the primal roots of the fear of looking stupid. It was probably some kind of survival mechanism when doing something different from the rest of the tribe was likely to cause a swift and gruesome death.

Tribal Jim: *You know, I've always wanted to cross the river and go talk to the people who live over there.*

Tribal Joan: *I wouldn't do that, you don't know what those people will do.*

Tribal Jim: *I'm sure it will be fine.*

Tribal Jim crosses the river and is greeted by a contingent of the "Across the River Tribe." Tribal Jim appears very different, as the members of the "This Side of the River" tribe wear their hair long, while the "Across the River Tribe" wears their hair short. They think Tribal Jim looks stupid so they cut off his head and mount it on a post, which is sign language that universally translates to "Please stay on your side of the river, hippies."

Hence, the fear of looking stupid. The perceived judgment of others holds us back from attempting all sorts of things. I will be mocked, I will be laughed at, I will be shamed, criticized, vilified. The fear of looking stupid holds us back from pursuing the things or even people we love. It makes us immobile, afraid to explore concepts and activities that attract a certain level of intellectual curiosity. The fear of looking stupid closes us off from whole worlds and groups of people who might lead us to new levels of happiness or education or health or wealth.

There are many books and experts that discuss fear and how to over-come it. My friend Patrick Sweeney, the "Fear Guru," is a perfect example of how one man faced a crippling fear, in his case of flying, and turned it around into an inspirational story. The fear that I am talk-ing about right now is specifically the fear of looking stupid. You cannot die from looking stupid. You cannot be physically injured by looking stupid. You can't accidentally slip or fall or poison yourself or sever a limb by looking stupid. These are all things that can actually happen in truly fear-inducing situations. Looking stupid? Generally speaking, the worst that happens is that you feel like a schmuck and people avoid making eye contact with you. While it may not feel great, it does not require a visit to the ER.

Yet this fear, unlike money or time or health, is 100 percent in our control. As much as I would like to think that I can walk out my front door and triple my income "Today! Using other people's money!" I rationally understand that there are many other forces and considerations that will factor into whether that can actually happen.

But fear of looking stupid? That is fully in my hands. If I want to run through the woods carrying a large branch and climb trees as a workout, or hide in the bushes to scare kids on Halloween, or use a glove to hold a cold pint of Ben and Jerry's Americone Dream, I can choose these things for myself, however "stupid" they appear to others. (Each of those examples is a real things that I do).

If I want to get up on stage and tell jokes, act out stories, collect albums from the dump, or buy "Dead Guy" suits, the only thing hold-ing me back is the opinion of others. And the fact of the matter is that I could give a rat's ass what anybody else thinks of me.

When you no longer particularly care what others think of you, it is one of the most liberating feelings in the world. No longer are you beholden to what others think or say about you. A huge psychic weight is lifted. You feel like a free pass has been given to you to explore all those oddball ideas or desires and dreams, no giving a damn what others think or say.

So how do you get to that place? It is fine and easy enough to say "Just do it" (trademark Nike, please don't sue me). Yet on a practical level that isn't usually how things work. Just like working out or physical fitness, one needs to build up strength and stamina to get to a place of doing things in a more extreme way. If you haven't run in years, you wouldn't go out and attempt a marathon. You would start with short runs and longer walks, building and compounding your efforts until the time when you can run a 5K, then a 10K, then a half marathon, then eventually a full marathon. Maybe you never run that full marathon, but you consistently and comfortable can run a 10K whenever you like. There is your win.

It is the same process for getting over the fear of looking stupid. Maybe you don't immediately hit the open mic stage, but rather you sign up for an improv class. That's all, just sign up. You don't even have to commit in your mind to go, just execute the simplest first step, which is signing up. You don't even need to tell anyone! Then once you do that, force yourself to go to the first class, no commitments after that.

What you will often find is that now you have put yourself in a situation where "looking stupid" isn't perceived as stupid at all, and what you are doing is actually the new normal. Sure, you are taking a risk by being in an improv class. But ultimately it is a very mitigated risk, because the entire environment is set up in such a way that everyone is facing that risk together.

Since everybody is facing the prospect of potentially looking stupid, ultimately no one does. As this new normal starts to feel more and more comfortable, you start to rewire your brain and how it perceives what is considered "stupid looking."

As you gradually develop these new thought patterns, you can start to apply that thinking wherever you like. That improv class may be just the thing to lead you to taking flying lessons, or dance lessons, or writing that book, or asking that guy/girl out for a beer. Because now your brain is starting to register that it isn't really that dangerous to look stupid, and the consequences of looking stupid are nowhere near as awful as we imagine.

Once that muscle becomes stronger, you start to want to use it more and more, flexing it wherever you damn well please. It becomes fun and actually validating when someone comments how stupid or crazy you look. When a person makes those kinds of comments to me about almost anything I am doing or thinking of doing, that is usually a sign that I am on the right path.

Hey, I get it. I don't blame you if you don't want to free-dive off of a cliff wearing a wing suit. Very bad things can happen that are far more serious then just enduring snarky comments behind your back.

What is even stupider than the fear of looking stupid is not pursuing those things in life that you want to try just because you are worried about what other people might think. So the practical steps you can take to overcome this fear? Take an improv class, or a beginner dance class, or join a reading or painting group or whatever you have an interest in. Put yourself out there in a smaller way to give yourself a core to build from. Constantly apply this approach and pretty soon you'll be experiencing a whole new life, making up all kinds of new shit that you never dreamed of before.

Chapter 6

People Don't Think about You as Much as You Think They Do

People are inherently narcissists. For now, we are all trapped in this one carbon-based body. (This should all the changing by 2050 with the coming of singularity, thank you very much, AI.) This means that each of us experiences the world through only one limited viewpoint. Our own.

It really does not matter how empathetic a person is or how considerate they are or how open to other perspectives a person may be. While all of those are admirable traits, it still does not change the fact that we can only perceive the world within our own brain. Life is our own film where we have a starring role and everybody else is a supporting character, at best.

Cynical? I don't think so. Clearly we need to think about ourselves more than anyone else on a day-to-day basis to actually stay alive. If we don't eat and drink and take all the other necessary steps as a human being on a regular basis, we will cease to exist. Fact, not opinion. We spend the majority of our time thinking about ourselves and what is necessary to do in order to, at the very least, function and, at the very best, be happy and healthy and thrive. If we accept that each person thinks mostly about his or her own self then we can infer that everyone else is thinking very little about us. And that is a liberating thing.

Comedians live and die by what people think about them. The reason that public speaking is consistently in the top three of the list of fears of human beings is because the fear of being humiliated in front of groups is a deep-seated primal emotion. A long time ago, being singled out and humiliated in front of your tribe or your village had very real consequences.

Being banished or burned at the stake or drowned as a witch were not emotional scars. They were very real and dangerous outcomes for people who were perceived as different. If you said to your friend in the Middle Ages, "Hey, dude, the king is full of shit, and I'm going to gather everybody at the village green and let them know all about it," your friend would likely reply, "Are you sure you want to do that? I mean, I don't disagree, but you might want to be careful about what you're saying."

So you go ahead and invite all of your friends and family to the village green to hear your thoughts on the king and why he is such a dink. A bunch of them show up out of a sense of obligation ("I'll go this one time and hopefully he will stop asking me to come see his shows"), while others are curious to hear what you have to say, and still others are hoping to see some kind of ox-drawn cart wreck (no trains, yet).

You really get going and you are just nailing the king. The guy is an idiot, doesn't care about the little people, is surrounded by sycophants, is fat, and can't sire a male heir. You know, classic "king" material. The audience is mostly with you, laughing and having a grand old time. Everybody but those two dudes standing in the front wearing long robes and pointy hats with their arms crossed. They don't seem to be digging your shtick. "Oh well, you can't please everybody," you think to yourself, and join up with your buddies at the local pub for an ale or two after the show.

Two days later you are in the castle dungeon being stretched on the rack as you confess to being possessed by evil spirits who are out to destroy the king.

Not a pleasant outcome for separating yourself from the crowd. In these times, caring about what other people thought of us was actually something that was important in terms of keeping ourselves alive. That feeling still exists in our brains today, but the physical danger is not nearly the same (except, of course, in countries that do not have freedom of speech, or on social media).

A comedian on stage will always have a residue of that primal fear. And while they learn to overcome and suppress it, there will always be the smallest kernel of fear or concern about the audience and whether or not they liked the show. I don't care how ballsy or confident a performer may be, somewhere deep in their lizard brains is a worry that the audience won't like them and that someone in that audience is going to report them to the king, and they'll end up being drawn and quartered.

The reality is that the audience really does not give nearly as much of a shit about the performer as the performer thinks they do. I have been performing, directing, or producing live comedy for over 20 years. Almost all audiences are the same in terms of how they respond to the performance. In general when people come out and see a good show their response is, "Hey, that was pretty funny, let's go out and get some drinks!" And when they see a bad show, their general response is," Hey, that was pretty bad, let's go out and get some drinks!"

It just doesn't matter to them the way it does to the performer. Good show or bad, the audience is quickly moving on with their lives, and what you did on the stage has very little impact not only on their life but in the immediate future of what they plan to do. They just aren't thinking about you as a performer the same way you think they are.

This, more than anything, is what good performers and public speakers and iconoclasts who do original things have mastered. The ability to not give a shit about what others think about them. And it is a relatively easy thing to do once we get in our heads that they are not thinking about us nearly as much as we think they are.

What that means for anybody who wants to do their own thing and blaze their own path is that we can and should ignore the concept of what other people think about us. Think about it like this; how much of your day is spent thinking about how stupid or awesome someone else is? Do you spend hours on end dissecting the words thoughts or actions of someone else? I highly doubt it.

You probably had passing thoughts regarding different people, but you most likely quickly moved on to more important thoughts like

"Should I get an Italian sub with extra hots for lunch today, or get a healthy green smoothie?" Since we know that other people spend a very small amount of their own personal time thinking about us, we therefore do not need to invest any of our own time thinking about what others think about us. It is a waste of time and, more important, erodes our self-confidence, stopping us from pursuing the things we want to do.

The fact that everybody is pretty much self-absorbed and mostly focusing on themselves is liberating. If we accept this fact, then it allows you to do whatever it is that strikes your fancy. By recognizing that your actions or ideas are not at the center of anybody else's concerns, you are freed up to explore your own pursuits. Other people no longer have power over how you approach creating new work. Now we can quickly move past the negative voices and self-doubt that will always creep into our heads.

There are plenty of ways to practice not giving a shit about what people think. What I have found helpful is to be declarative in anything that I'm doing. In improv we are trained to make declarative statements wherever possible. This helps drive the action in the scene and also to make very clear to our scene partner as well as the audience what we are trying to achieve.

Strong declarative statements help narrow and control the narrative. Where the possibilities can lead are endless in improv – to have a coherent scene we have to carve away the other possibilities and eventually settle on an agreed subject.

For example, a general statement could be "What do you want to do?" While this kind of open-ended question can lead to thousands of different responses, it also gives the power of the narrative over to the other actor, who has to respond. Oftentimes the responding actor assumes the actor who initiated the dialogue has something in mind and responds with something like, "I don't know, what do you want to do?" This is just about as bad a beginning to an improv scene as you can get. Vague statements with no actions being taken by anyone.

This is what a declarative statement would look like: "Let's grab a coffee at Dunk's." This is a strong statement that gives the other actor and the audience clear understanding of the first actor's intent.

Actor number 2 now just needs to respond one way or the other and does not have to guess what actor number 1 wants or is thinking.

Easy enough to do on stage, but what does that look like in real life? If we are not caring about what other people think, making declarative statements allows the individual to control the narrative of the conversation and clarifies how they feel about something without ever having to be asked. For example, imagine this conversation:

John: *I was thinking about taking a yoga class*
Dan: *Why? Are you getting all New Age-y now? People look stupid doing yoga and you wouldn't know any of the moves.*

Besides discovering that Dan is a super-negative turd of a friend, it is easy to see how criticism and self-doubt could creep into John's thought processes as to whether he should or shouldn't take a yoga class. The same conversation using declarative statements looks like this:

John: *So, I'm taking yoga now.*
Dan: *Since when did you get so New Age-y?*
John: *It helps me with my flexibility and it settles my mind. It is hard but so far I have loved doing it.*
Dan: *Good for you. Hey, want to go grab some drinks?*

I have often found that making a strong declarative statement along the lines of "So, I'm doing X now," tends to stop other people from offering overly negative judgments about what it is I'm doing. It is easy for people to point out why you shouldn't begin something, but it is much more difficult for people to tell you why you should stop doing something, especially if you follow up with the reason why you like doing it. Even the biggest blowhard tends to not want to crush someone else's good vibes.

The declarative statement takes the power of judgment away from the responder. Once you state what it is you are doing, most people tend to shrug their shoulders and think to themselves," I guess she is doing that now." They may approve or disapprove, but ultimately if they see that you are already committed, they tend to move on to other subjects.

Strong declarative statements don't require a ton of follow-up expla-nations. They lay out why you are doing something or why you feel a certain way.

John: *I have given up eating red meat.*
Dan: *Why? You love burgers and steaks.*
John: *It makes me feel better and give me more energy.*
Dan: *Well, good for you! Hey, want to go grab some drinks?*

Why is Dan such a negative twit? He just brings everybody down and clearly has a drinking problem. From a functional standpoint, declar-ative statements shut down negative statements and send the message that you are not overly interested about how the other person feels about what you are doing. By practicing this technique you start to develop somewhere in your brain the ability to care less and less about what people think. This in turn removes one of the biggest obstacles to creating or being original thinker.

Another fun little technique that you can practice is responding to negative thoughts or opinions with two simple words, "Thank you."

Saying "Thank you" to a negative statement completely disarms the person who is making it. It is also a confident but not super-aggressive way to demonstrate that you do not give a shit about what the other person thinks and it really doesn't bother you that they don't agree with you. For example:

Kira: *That jacket looks stupid on you.*
Ashley: *Thank you.*

Kira is now confused and knocked off balance. She just insulted Ashley and didn't get anywhere near the response that she was expect-ing. Kira could come back with another insulting remark and Ashley can continue to respond with things like "Thank you, I appreciate it." Very quickly, Kira will stop offering these negative critiques and move on because it will quickly become apparent that Ashley is not affected by Kira's opinion and has no interest in having a discussion.

It is so simple and effective and very clearly communicates that you do not need someone else's validation of your own thoughts and ideas.

The conversation will quickly shift on to other things, most likely revolving around Kira's life and problems, because ultimately most people just want to talk about themselves.

What has become harder in today's day and age is the explosion of social media and other forums where individuals can critique you. Because those opinions stay online, they feel all the more real and powerful. There are millions of digital opinion warriors ready to tear down anyone for anything at anytime.

One response would be: "Stay off and away from any sites and forums that have that kind of toxic culture. It is a world you can actively choose not to be in if it is causing you any kind of stress." I truly believe this. You would not go to a gym if every time you went in, everyone started to tell you that you are fat and out of shape. You would never go to a movie theater if as soon as you bought tickets to a movie, people in the lobby starting shouting at you about what an idiot you are for choosing that film. Why the hell would anyone subject themselves to the same kind of treatment online?

Of course social media and digital discourse is never going away, so basically becoming an Internet Hermit is not really a viable choice for most of us. The good thing about the internet and social media is that, just like discussions in the biological world, people mostly care about themselves and quickly move on to other things if they are not engaged.

The only person whose opinion truly matters in regards to what you are creating is your own. At least in the initial phases. Sure, at some point, if you've created material for public consumption, other people's opinions will matter in the moment. But even then, whether they deem what you created is good or bad, they will look at each other and say, "Hey, you want to go grab some drinks?"

Chapter 7

Facing Failure: Be Wrong to Be Right

Sometimes you have to be wrong to be right. Making shit up also means that plenty of shit goes wrong. One of the hardest things to get comfortable with as a leader as well as a creator is admitting that you are wrong. It can be a scary thing, and, let's face it, doesn't feel good. You can feel pretty damn stupid at times.

Failure is an undeniable part of any creative process. There's no such thing as a perfectly formed and executable idea. Where something begins is never where it ends, no matter the initial spark of genius that ignites the idea. Iterating, failing, and advancing the concept are all part of the process of making stuff up.

There are many experts who can speak on the various different ideas around failure – failing fast, failing forward, failing early, and failing often. I come at it from the perspective of playing make pretend on stage and trying to get people to laugh at my nonsense. While I agree with every one of those types of failure, only in comedy do you experience all of those again and again, night after night in front of people who immediately let you know that you are in fact failing. A comedian failing on stage is not a theoretical endeavor. It is a very real and tangible thing. And it can leave marks.

The beauty of this kind of failure is that like real bodily injuries you start to build up psychic scar tissue. I have never met a single person in this industry who has not bombed on stage. Anyone who has ever done comedy, no matter what level they have achieved, has spent a significant amount of time being painfully unfunny in front of people. Some find their funny and their voice faster than others, but the fact remains that when you are creating something out of nothing and trying to elicit an emotional response from people, you can only figure it out through trial and error.

I think at this point most people understand that failure is necessary. What I want to discuss is the idea that the fear of failure can be overcome and does not need to stop you from pursuing your dreams. Tolerance to failure can be built up just like tolerance to physical pain, exercising, or heat or cold or alcohol. And the way you build a tolerance is by repeated exposure to the thing you want immunity from.

Coming up as a comedian has helped to build within myself a resiliency against failure. When you allow yourself to fail again and again on stage you begin find that the actual act of failing becomes less and less painful and important. By failing a whole bunch of times in a low-stakes environment – in my instance on open mic stages in crappy bars and clubs around Boston – you begin to develop that scar tissue.

As that scar tissue becomes thicker, you feel the pain less and less. As the pain subsides, so does your fear. As your fear goes down, your confidence in what you are doing correspondingly goes up. As your confidence grows, you begin to associate pleasure with the act for taking risks and creating. Your mind starts to comprehend that small short-term failures aren't really setbacks at all, and that as long as you keep pushing forward and putting in the reps, you are bound to get stronger at whatever it is that you are doing.

The fear of failure is right up there with the fear of looking stupid in terms of things that we can control and often stop us from moving ahead with our ideas and dreams. Especially in the beginning stages of any new endeavor, pushing through our own fear of failure is pretty much up to us.

I clearly remember the first open mic comedy set I ever did. I knew I wanted to try stand-up comedy. I first started by taking small actions that were within my control and that had very little risk. I found out where the open mics were. I went to see some shows. I started writing down my ideas in a notebook. All of these actions that I could take really didn't expose me to any sort a failure.

I didn't have to tell anyone I was doing any of these things, so there was no judgment from others that I had worry about. Since each of these actions was personal and private, there were no consequences good or bad that came from them.

I finally mustered up the courage to take the critical step from being a passive observer and private creator to putting my thoughts and actions out there in the public realm. I got the number of the person who booked the open mic acts at Dick Doherty's Comedy Vault, a comedy club in the basement of Remington's restaurant on Boylston Street in Boston. It was called The Vault because the basement had once been a bank vault, and the huge mechanized door with all of its wheels and gears was still there in the basement. I wrote, prepared, and did my five minutes along with 18 other people on the bill that night. It predictably went about as well as you'd expect from a person who had never done standup comedy before in their life. That is to say, I sucked and wasn't particularly funny.

I remember hanging out for a while after the show and eventually making my way to the exit where, with my tail between my legs, I thanked the organizer for giving me a chance. The guy, barely looking up from his binder, gave me a quick look and said "Not bad for your first time. I have a spot next month if you want it."

I was shocked. I figured this was my one shot, and that I had failed so badly and so publicly there was no way I was going to be invited back to perform. As I took the Green Line trolley back to my pantry apartment in Cleveland Circle, something clicked in my head. It occurred to me that as long as I was willing to get back onstage, they were willing to let me get back on stage. I came to understand that the organizer of the show didn't particularly care if I failed, and that if I didn't care if I failed, then there was no barrier to keep me from performing.

Now of course this was the appropriate setting for where I was in my own skill set, and the consequences of my failure were really just my own ego in psychic pain. I kept getting back up there on that stage and, needless to say, I improved. I was doing the same thing with improv groups around the city as well. If somebody would let me improvise with them, then I did it. It made no difference to me if I was good or they were good or an audience thought that I/we were good. I was willing to fail, and then try to dissect the feedback regarding what worked and what didn't and improve from one show to the next.

Developing the ability to push through the fear of failure has helped me far beyond anything I've ever done on the stage. At some point it becomes relatively easy to create onstage. No matter how big a show is, the stakes are in all actuality pretty low. They think you are funny or they don't, they go out for drinks either way, and some portion of the audience is willing to come back and see another show and some won't. Nobody dies or loses their life savings and we all get on with our lives.

This isn't exactly the case when you're creating or taking risks in the "real world." There clearly can be far greater consequences and therefore the idea of failing can be far more daunting. But the tolerance that I built up to risk and failure has served me incredibly well as I have helped conceive, develop, and grow my businesses. By building up that scar tissue I have been able to move through the fear of failure in many different areas of my life.

The creation of Improv Asylum is a perfect example. When I and my two partners at the time identified that we had a chance to take over a 200-seat theater and bar in the heart of Boston's North End, the only thing that was holding us back was the idea that it may not work.

At the time, improv comedy was not known as a popular commercial entertainment form. There was no successful precedent for this kind of business in Boston. Nobody was shouting from the rooftop "Lord, please bring us live improv comedy, we the masses demand it!"

The odds of failure were great and in fact most everybody expected we would. And why wouldn't they? I was a 26-year-old who lived in a pantry and was so broke that I my car had recently been repossessed. There wasn't a lot of there to indicate that a stellar career in entertainment and business lay ahead of me.

What was very clear to the three of us, though, was the idea that we wanted to find out if this would work or not. All of us agreed that when we were 40 we wanted to know that it was either a success or a failure. What we couldn't live with was the idea of not trying and having to wonder what might've been.

Being "wrong" is different from failing. A decision can still be right even if it fails. Because I love football and belabored sports analogies, consider a coach's decision to go for it on fourth and two. If the team picks up the two yards, they can run out the clock and win the game. If it doesn't, they give the ball back to their opponent who still has time to march down the field to potentially win. Going for it on fourth and two may still be the "right" decision even if the team fails to pick up the two yards. The lack of execution may result in the "failure" to pick up the first down, but the decision to go for it is not necessarily "wrong."

Being "wrong" typically means that upon reflection you would do something differently, or that an outcome that you were very sure was going to happen didn't materialize. Failure is something we can live with. We learn from our mistakes and hopefully improve from this new knowledge. Being wrong? That's personal. Being wrong feels much more like a critique of our talent, intelligence, or moral compass. Saying "I failed" implies that you at least tried. Being "wrong" just seems like you are an idiot. Nobody likes to feel like an idiot.

But when you open yourself up to acknowledging you were wrong about something – a decision, idea or concept – you open yourself to being right. Other, better options often appear. You learn something new from being wrong as well. Things become clearer and you begin to understand concepts that you may not have before. Being wrong allows you to definitively eliminate certain things and focus on the ideas or actions that are working.

Admitting that you are wrong, as anybody who has had a romantic relationship with anybody already knows, can be incredibly difficult. What is also true is that usually, by that simple admission, the problem is defused and solutions begin to present themselves.

For me, this happened 19–20 years into the life of Improv Asylum. And I am not talking about some creative concept or show idea. I'm talking about very real world stuff. As my companies have grown in size, scope, and complexity I had been resistant to adding in more controls, specifically HR controls. My attitude had always been "We don't need that. It will kill the culture of creativity and freewheel-ing exchange and development of ideas. We create comedy, for shit's sake, now we are going to have HR telling us what to do and say? No thanks."

Good people, people with whom I had worked closely for 20 years and who are smart and talented told me many times that we should do more, that the company was growing and in need of this kind of support. Employees as well. Great people who cared about the company as much as I did. And yet I didn't listen. I knew better. Or at least I didn't want to face the fact that if we needed that kind of support, then that meant I, too, probably needed to change the way I was doing certain things.

You change, sure. Me, change? No thank you very much. It was easiest to hide behind the mantra of "HR will change the culture for the worse."

I was wrong. We needed to grow. The company we owned at 20 years was not the same company it had been at 1, 5, 10, or even 15 years. It was different. I was different. Unfortunately, it took several difficult incidents to galvanize me into action. But once I decided that I was wrong and we needed to change and seriously look at what we were doing with this segment of the company, I was all in.

And then a funny thing happened. That thing that I feared, the culture changing, started to happen. The culture definitely started changing. For the better. I could feel it. I could see it and hear it. And I started to change too, for the better. This thing that I feared, HR for more professionalism and structure, things that I thought were overrated and not all that important, became far less scary. I started working with amazing professionals outside the company who showed me so much more than I ever thought was important on that side of the business. I started to learn again. I was getting coaching, notes, ideas from incredible people who knew a hell of a lot more than I did about this stuff.

Here is the scary part. I liked it. I mean, like really, really enjoyed it. I never thought that I, as a guy who came up in comedy, who went into comedy and started businesses because I didn't want to listen to or be like other people, would totally dig having deep philosophical conversations about HR, culture, employees, and all the things that come with this subject. No one wanted to "change" our culture in a negative way, they wanted to help make what we have at this stage in the company's life much, much better. That became something I could get excited by. Why the hell wouldn't I want to get better, both personally and as a business leader?

I was wrong. I feel stupid looking at it now and realizing that I should have embraced a new way of thinking long ago. I'm stubborn, confident in my ideas, always convinced I can figure it out. Great traits to have as an entrepreneur most of the time.

Being willing to be wrong proved to be more important than any of those characteristics at this point in my company's history. By being wrong, I was able to look at things in a whole new way. It has given me a brand-new confidence in what I'm doing and where I know my companies can go.

Admitting you are wrong is hard. Change is hard. We still have a long way to go and I know I'll screw plenty of things up along the way. And when I do, I'll have no problem admitting that I was wrong. Because it will give me the opportunity to be right again.

"Great story, dude. But what the hell can I do to feel more comfortable with the fear of failure and admitting when I am wrong?" you aggressively ask.

Let's take a look at some very simple actions or exercises you can take to build up your own psychic scar tissue. Again, I am biased, but enrolling in an improv class is hands-down the most tangible way to safely experience the fear of failure. While the emotional and physical response to that fear will be very real, the stakes are actually quite low. Lower even than any kind of public performance.

By putting yourself in an improv environment you'll gain tangible experience pushing through the fear of failure and realizing that failure isn't the end of the world. And I can almost guarantee that wherever you are, there is an improv class being taught somewhere nearby. If there isn't, contact me, no matter where you are or what country you live in, and we will figure something out.

While my specialty is improv, you could choose any number of new skills that will flex your psychic muscles. Take an acting class or dance lessons. Join a painting group or take a public speaking course. Sign up for scuba-diving classes at your local YMCA or beginner rock-climbing classes at your local rock gym.

Basically, explore any activity that is tangible that you have never done before. Going to a lecture or a talk doesn't count because this is a passive activity and you do not get the firsthand experience of doing it.

You will experience some sort of a failure in anything new that you try, and that is a good thing. Because the consequences are, well, inconsequential in any kind of beginning class, this will allow you to experience and push through small failures. These first-hand experiences will start to rewire your brain and how you experience and think about failure.

So how does one practice being wrong? I would suggest that it's not about practicing being wrong, it is about practicing *admitting* when we are wrong. And that can be done simply by stating or writing down "I was wrong" whenever we are incorrect. For example, how often have you been in this scenario:

Lisa: *Take the next right and the restaurant will be about a mile down on your left.*
Dana: *I'm pretty sure it is a left at the lights.*
Lisa: *It's not, it is definitely a right.*

This mini argument goes on for a little while and it turns out that Dana is correct, it was a left at the lights. Instead of saying what most people will typically say, "Huh, I thought it was a right" or maybe a begrudging "You were right," here is a chance to simply say "I was wrong."

It may seem incredibly simplistic, but by finding basic things that you are wrong about and ideally verbalizing them (another way to do this is to keep a running list in a notebook or your phone or wherever the hell you keep your notes) helps take the self-conscious sting out of admitting we were mistaken about something. Verbalizing or writing down "I was wrong" helps us to be more comfortable with the idea of not always having to be right.

It completely decreases the time and energy we waste arguing over inconsequential details or about things that don't really matter much. When you say "I was wrong" in almost any argument, it completely diffuses the situation and brings an end to the conflict. Once the admission has been made, the other party typically quickly settles down and looks to find a solution or way forward. And making shit up requires that we move forward and not dwell too long on the past or get stuck in the present.

Another occurrence that happens is that when you say "I was wrong," the other person often becomes conciliatory and may minimize your mistake.

Lisa: *I was wrong, it was a left.*
Dana: *I get that turn screwed up all the time, no worries.*

So here are your marching orders: Sign up for an activity that you haven't done before, and find daily small things that you are wrong about, and say out loud or write down in your notes, "I was wrong about X."

These simple things, which in many cases cost zero dollars, are within your control. And if you do take these steps, you will begin to see that the fear of failure and of being wrong are barriers that we place in front ourselves. Since we put those obstacles there, we have the ability to remove them, as well.

Chapter 8

Heightening

In improv comedy, the actors are making up scenes and stories from nothing. They start by showing up and stepping out on that stage. They don't know what they're going to do or say, nor do they know what their fellow actors are going to do or say. Standing on a floor-level stage in a dark basement theater, the actors are surrounded on all sides by an audience that is in parts excited, indifferent, supportive and hostile.

The actor, standing alone on stage with the rest of the cast behind him/her, asks the audience a simple question, something like "What have you recently purchased for over $100?" Without any preplanned thoughts or conversations, these actors take the rawest of material and weave a tale with multiple layers, many different characters, jumps in time, unexpected twists and turns, all somehow leading to a neat resolution of the story. When done well, it feels almost like a magic trick. Six performers, never speaking a word to each other, somehow immediately get on the same page, coherently moving ideas forward so seamlessly that it looks like it must be preplanned.

In a matter of seconds, improv actors have to accept a previously unknown idea, free associate off of what they have heard, negotiate with another actor as to the who, what, and where of the scene, come to an agreement, and move the idea forward. All while also attempting to make the audience laugh. The performers are also being publicly judged, and the feedback that they receive tells them if they have been successful or if they have failed almost immediately.

So how, exactly, do these people create in such a stressful environment? Is it natural talent? A divine spark? Extreme narcissism, an expression of risk-taking, or the need to be loved by a group of strangers? It is really none of those things (Well, except perhaps the narcissism and the need to be loved). What improvisational actors are doing is using a highly advanced communication skill set that they have practiced and honed over many years, a skill set that allows them to exchange information with each other in such a way that moves ideas forward, while also letting the ideas evolve throughout the scene. Improv actors have mastered the ability to listen to other people's ideas while also having the confidence to add their own input to help advance the scene. The end product is a wholly original piece of work that no one performer can claim credit for, yet each actor can call their own.

Creating in this way is not just attainable by the actors on stage but really by anyone who wants to learn the improvisational process. It is a process that can be broken down into different parts and applied to most any creative endeavor. While there are many books about the high philosophy and deep art of improv, I try to look at things in a more functional way. We can discuss theory all day long, what I really want to know if I'm reading this book is the tangible things I can do to make shit up. So let's explore.

We have already covered the importance of listening. Without this basic fundamental skill, you will be shit out of luck trying to implement these other techniques. I cannot emphasize enough the importance of listening to understand and how that will positively impact everything else you do in life. We have discussed the idea jumping on the spark when we see it. Being able to create an environment where inspiration can find us is critical. Through curiosity, observing and doing shit we constantly expose ourselves to new stimuli that will eventually show itself to us and the form of a spark of inspiration. We have practiced overcoming our of fear of looking stupid as well overcoming our fear of failure. Now let's take a look and how we can make shit up and move ideas forward in a real way.

Once we have identified an idea that excites us and just won't go away, we need to do something about it. After the initial euphoria of the new idea wears off, the daunting reality sets in: "How am I ever going to make this thing happen?"

The first thing I like to do is heighten the concept. "Heightening" is a technique where a concept is built upon in such a way that it grows from a seemingly normal, practical idea into a crazy, outlandish end product that makes people lose their minds. This is the most fun part of the process. We are allowing our imagination to go places that are exciting and original, unfettered by practicality or reality at the moment.

In an improv scene heightening is what builds the stakes and tension and generally leads to humor. If a scene consists of someone walking into a coffee shop, purchasing a cup of coffee, and then leaving, it would be fairly uninteresting. A version of that scene with heightening might look like this:

Someone walks into a coffee shop to purchase a cup of coffee. Upon receiving their cup of coffee the person is informed that they are the one-millionth customer. Excited, the customer asks if they get a free cup of coffee. The barista says no. The barista then points out the window to a dump truck filled with one million coffee beans, exclaiming that the beans are the prize! The customer is so excited that they run out the door to see what they have won. The guy in the dump truck sees the customer come out of the store and asks if they are the winner. The customer says yes, and the truck driver immediately dumps all one million coffee beans on the customer, burying him.

As you can see, the heightening that happened in this scene led to a far more interesting and hopefully funny story. The same original premise was still there – customer walks into a coffee shop to buy a cup of coffee – but by making exaggerated choices at different parts in the scene, it became far more compelling to watch.

That is all well and good when done onstage, but what does it look like with ideas that are not performance related?

Here is an example of a general idea, heightened:

I'm interested in rescue dogs.
What if I rescue stray dogs?
What if I create a home for them?

What if that home was a farm?

How about a ranch?

10 acres.

50 acres.

100 acres.

1,000 acres.

A ranch where hundreds of dogs could live.

Thousands of dogs.

And I call it Dogland Ranch.

And that ranch is on a tropical island, because I want to live somewhere warm.

And it becomes a destination where people who love animals can
spend a week living with the dogs, tending to them and just enjoying helping the animals.

And at the end of their stay they can adopt a dog.

And I build a hotel and resort for them to stay at while visiting.

And I build a veterinary clinic, where not only are the animals taken
cared for but training is also provided for the local population.

And I team up with a renowned veterinary school in the United
States to make it happen.

And also on that land I develop other businesses.

A winery: Dogland Ranch wines.

A distillery: Dogland Ranch Rum.

A legal marijuana farm: Dogland Ranch Best Buds.

And profits from these other industries go to saving more animals
and educating more people.

That is what heightening looks like, and for me it is easily the most
fun part of the creative process. (Full disclosure, this is an idea I'm
actively working on. If anybody reading this has 1,000 acres available
on a tropical island, hit me up. Dogland Ranch is my retirement plan.)
I am of the belief that it takes just about the same amount of effort to
think big as it does to think small. If I am going to exert my admittedly
limited mental energy, I might as well have fun and think big.

What heightening an idea does is create excitement and momentum, and the further you go with it the looser and less judgmental you
become. As you become less judgmental you allow ideas to blossom

that maybe you might not have considered or would have quickly discarded in the past.

What may seem ridiculous if thought of on its own now fits perfectly into the flow of the heightening process. By heightening the original ideas, you now have far more material to consider. Your original idea is still there and you can go back to it at any point, but you also may find that you have new or more interesting versions of that original concept that excite you. You can then go back to the list you have created and start to consider what path you want to take and which ideas seem feasible.

Maybe a hotel and resort on a tropical island is not attainable. But maybe a small bed-and-breakfast with a barn and 30 acres is. An entire veterinary clinic may be out of reach, but a local partnership with an area university might be just the thing. A marijuana farm might be unrealistic due to legal restrictions, but a craft distillery branded with your business and the profits going to a great cause may be the perfect combination of seemingly unrelated ideas. Now we have enough of an idea that we can start to take basic actions to begin moving it forward.

Practicing heightening is the easiest and most fun thing to do in the entire creative process. As ideas come to you, simply play the what-if game. Start with your original concept and ask "What if…," adding on an ending to the question. Build each "What if…" question off of the last one. By doing it this way, you begin to stack ideas, building a tower of loosely connected concepts. The ideas at the top of the tower may not seem to have any connection to the original idea. That is perfectly okay and actually desired. But because each idea is built off of the one that precedes it, you can easily trace back from top to bottom and recognize unseen connections.

Like all of the concepts we are discussing in this book, the more you practice these techniques, the easier they are to perform. You can do this kind of exercise alone or in a group, anywhere at anytime, for zero dollars.

Chapter 9

Yes and, Maybe, No

If you want to make shit up for a living in this world, you need to understand a few things about how people communicate with each other. Words have meaning, yes. They also have a great power and influence. The words we choose have immense impact on how we create.

Verbal communication is the number-one way to exchange information and ideas with other people on a day-to-day basis. What we say and how we say it completely determines whether or not we can successfully get our ideas into action. You can be the most brilliant person in the world, but if you can never communicate your ideas, there is really nothing we can do with them.

Communication is the secret sauce of success. Think of it this way: All things being close to equal, would you prefer having a doctor who is a poor communicator or a doctor who is a great communicator? That same concept applies in any job. Who wins, the coder or the coder who is a great communicator? The teacher or the teacher who is a great communicator? The mechanic or the mechanic who is a great communicator? And so on and so on.

There is almost never a time when, given the opportunity to choose, someone would ever say, "Given the choice, I'll take the poor communicator." Just doesn't happen. Effective communication completely changes the game in terms of how people view you both personally and professionally. The better communicator you become, the better your personal and professional relationships will be.

When we improvise onstage, we are using a well-honed communication skill set that the audience never really sees. Hopefully the actors just look brilliant and funny and incredibly fast on their feet. We want the audience to laugh and be entertained and constantly be surprised and delighted by our choices onstage.

We want to leave them amazed and asking "How do they think so fast to come up with that stuff?" You do not necessarily want them to see the underlying skill set that the actors are using to communicate with each other, which is being able to quickly get on the same page and advance ideas. In general, we don't want you to see how the sausage is made; we just want you to enjoy the delicious, unhealthy sausage.

All communication can be broken down into three avenues of approach; yes, no, or maybe. Do you love me? Yes, no, maybe. You want to grab a beer? Yes, no, maybe. Should we colonize Mars, or get sushi tonight, go for a walk or buy a dog or any other situation you can think of, the communication comes down to yes, no, or maybe.

There are no emotional connotations to these words. "Yes" is not a good word and "no" is not a bad word. Each has power and influence regarding how ideas are or are not moved forward. Since this book is meant primarily for people interested in creating ideas and moving them forward, let's take a look at the impact these words have on this process.

NO

No. Say it out loud. *No!* You can feel the power in this simplest of words. No is authority. No is discipline, the parent, the teacher. No by its nature is negative. No is often fearful, afraid of change. No is risk-averse, happy to maintain the status quo. No is safe. No can be knee-jerk. No is hard to hear and easy to say. No also has great power. It can be decisive and strong.

No has the ability to stop unwanted actions in their tracks. No can be rebellious and brave, empowering people to stand up for themselves and what they believe. No can be hard to say, as it often disappoints. Used correctly, no can help shape the creative process. Wielded in a haphazard way, no can stop the creative process before it ever gets a chance to begin.

The idea of "No" has great influence on the creative process, especially at the beginning. In improv we are taught to avoid saying "No," especially at the very beginning of the scene. If an improv actor offers an idea and their scene partner immediately says "No" to it, then that scene is effectively over. At the very least it has to be restarted by one or another of those actors. Here is an example of a "No" scene:

Gabby: *Hey, you want to grab a cup of coffee?*
Lucy: *No, I don't like coffee.*

I have seen this scene 10,000 times from beginning improvisers (and from far too many experienced ones as well). On a basic level it doesn't really seem that bad. Gabby asks a question, Lucy says "No." The problem is that from a creative standpoint we have nowhere to go. Either Gabby have to try to convince Lucy to go get a cup of coffee or she needs to offer an alternative. Lucy, on the other hand, is making her scene partner do all the work.

Lucy can just sit there and force Gabby to keep coming up with ideas that Lucy can shoot down or at the very least pick and choose from, passing judgment on which ideas she thinks are good. The functional problem here is that going for coffee may be Gabby's only idea. Once Lucy says "No," Gabby might have nothing else to offer, and then the two actors just stand there staring at each other onstage, flop-sweat beading on their brow and a pit of panic spreading in their guts.

A more likely scenario might go like this:

Gabby: *Hey, you want to grab a cup of coffee?*
Lucy: *No, I don't like coffee.*
Gabby: *You drink coffee all the time.*
Lucy: *I never drink coffee.*
Gabby: *I saw you at Dunkin' Donuts yesterday.*
Lucy: *I have never been to a Dunkin' Donuts in my life.*
Gabby: *Are you calling me a liar?*
Lucy: *Are you saying I am lying?*

I have seen a version of this scene so many times that it makes me want to jab my eyes out just thinking about it. If you thought it was not entertaining reading that scene, it is 100 times worse watching it. As a viewer it becomes awkward and uncomfortable to watch two people argue over such a trivial detail at the very beginning of the scene.

Saying "No" at the very beginning of the scene also tends to leads directly to an argument or one-on-one conflict. While this can get laughs at first, they will quickly die out as the audience becomes frustrated that no new information is being added and that the story isn't going anywhere. Here is another way this scene typically goes:

Gabby: *Want to grab a cup of coffee?*
Lucy: *No, I don't drink coffee. Let's go get some tea.*
Gabby: *Tea is gross. I hate tea.*

No begets no, negative begets negative.

It is human nature for us to defend our ideas. When we take that risk and offer our idea to the world, or in this case our scene partner, we have left ourselves vulnerable. When our idea is immediately denied, not only does this stop the potential for any action, it also stings a little and puts us on the defensive. More often than not, when our partner offers an alternative idea we end up shooting it down and sticking to our initial position.

In improvisation we know this to be true; saying "no" at the very beginning of a scene stops the action from moving forward. There is nothing for us to explore if we come out of the gate just saying "no." There are no new possibilities and nothing to discover if we are stopping the action, shutting ideas down at the very beginning of the process. We also know that if you say "No" to someone else's idea in the initial stages of ideation you are incentivizing them to say no to any idea that you may offer back. If you pitch me on an idea and I say no, and then I pitch you on my idea, human nature more often than not will have you point out the flaws in my idea, or the very least how my idea is no better than yours. We now have created an antagonistic environment where we are no longer sharing ideas, we are arguing our points and shooting each other's offers down.

Saying "No" leads to uninteresting and uncomfortable scenes. Not only that, but it begins to break down the cohesion of the ensemble. We see this all too often: If Lucy is constantly shooting Gabby's ideas down, the next time Lucy goes out on stage to start a scene, Gabby will be inclined to stay back. Why should Gabby go out and enter the scene if she knows her ideas are going to be shot down? She will let somebody else deal with that BS. Or, Gabby will go out and let Lucy have the first line of dialogue and then Gabby will negate Lucy's idea and get a laugh at Lucy's expense. All this leads to great mistrust between the actors on stage and breaks down the ability to work effectively with each other.

And let's talk about that negative laugh for a second. Can you get laughs out of negation or saying no? Of course you can. The problem arises when people have to have repeated interactions with each other. If one actor is always getting laughs at the other performer's expense, that actor starts to separate themselves from the group. In a team setting, no individual likes to constantly be the butt of someone else's joke.

When one person is constantly bearing the brunt of other people's jokes, that is an indication that there's a huge status and respect problem. I hear it all the time from companies that I work with: "Oh, everybody gives Tom shit all the time. He knows we do it because we love him, he doesn't mind."

I guarantee you that Tom does mind. He may not say anything to you and may go along with the joke, but on the inside no person likes to constantly be made fun of or be demeaned, especially in front of others.

If this kind of joking is coming from a boss to an employee or a manager to subordinate, it is all the more problematic because the status of the relationship means that the lower-status person cannot equally joke back in the same negative way. Being negative is often couched in phrases like "I'm just a sarcastic person" or "I like to give people shit, it's the way I show affection."

This kind of humor works great among friends or peer sets because typically everyone holds fairly equal positions. I can give my buddy shit because he knows he can give it right back to me and there are no outside consequences. There is an element of trust that has been built up over years with your friends that allows you to be a little rougher with each other, because you know how you feel about each other on a deeper level. This is typically not the case in teams that have been put together from the outside.

One of the worst places where I see this behavior is in coaching of youth sports. Adults seem to think that a great way to connect with kids is by being sarcastic. It is generally one of the worst ways to forge a connection with a kid. First and foremost, the power dynamic is way off. Almost no kid has the confidence or the wherewithal to give shit back to a coach. To the contrary, if they do, they are considered disrespectful. Second, kids do not understand the nuances of sarcasm. When someone misses a fly ball and the coach yells out, "Hey, you know you're supposed to catch that, right?" The kid doesn't register that comment in their as yet unfully formed brain as humor. They register it as humiliation.

Yes, as you get to know your players and a bond is created, then of course you have some leeway to joke around and be sarcastic. But even then, if not used correctly with clear intent that you do not really mean it, sarcasm usually comes across as the coach just being shitty and making the player feel bad. I suppose if you think that making a player feel bad increases their chances of doing what you want more effectively, then by all means, be a sarcastic dick. Just be aware that modern social science does not back up this theory.

When we say "No" to one idea we are typically saying no to three, four, or five ideas. What I mean by this is that if you come to pitch me an idea and I say no to you, you may come back with a second idea. If I say "No" to the second idea and point out that it is not very good, what are the odds that you are going to come to me with ideas three, four, and five? Not very good. More often than not the person pitching the idea will think, No, thanks, I don't need that kind of humiliation again after the first couple of ideas.

Here is the issue: Ideas one and two may suck, but in ideas three, four, or five, there may be one that is brilliant. Yet I will never get to hear them if I just say "No" at the very beginning of the idea exchange.

It is very important that I point out that we are talking about the "ideation" phase and not the "execution" phase. In the ideation phase we are looking to explore new possibilities. We want to add raw material into the ideation gristmill to get things churning. As we get to the execution phase, then we will need to start saying no and eliminating concepts that we don't think will work. By listening and encouraging the team to offer ideas in the initial stages, team members will be more likely to understand if their idea is not selected and be more inclined to buy-in on the final decision.

I absolutely do not discount the power and importance of "No." At some point in the decision-making process, possibilities need to be eliminated and a course of action needs to be set. "No" can be empowering, especially when used to stop unwanted actions from moving forward. We see this in dealing with children, particularly at-risk youths. With this group it is important that we teach them how to say "No." As we all know, teenagers are at the stage in their lives when they are facing a lot of choices, many of which are risky and with which they have no experience. In these instances it becomes important to explain that "No" is a valid and important choice in keeping themselves safe and away from things that may be harmful to them.

"No" is also an important choice for groups who have been marginalized or victimized. By saying "No" they show they will no longer stand being treated in a certain way. By making a firm stand, a group can claim control of their future.

Finally, it's not about *never* saying "No," but rather choosing how and when you say "No." It is an important part of the creative process. The key to understanding "No" is communicating the "why" of the "no."

Improv Asylum has done a lot of work with Red Bull, the energy-drink company. Periodically we are asked to work with their sampling teams. Now, folks on their sampling teams have a tough gig. Their job is to hit the streets and try to get people to sample Red Bull. As you might expect, they face a lot of rejection and negativity. Coupled with the fact that most of the people that make up these teams are usually between 18 and 21 and don't have a ton of professional communication training, it is easy to see how some issues may arise.

We went out into the field and observed how the Red Bull sampling teams work. The typical interaction went something like this:

Red Bull team member: *Hi, would you like to try a Red Bull?*
Customer: *No, thanks, I heard that Red Bull is loaded with caffeine.*
Red Bull team member: *No it's not, you should try it.*
Customer: *Yeah, it is, and I don't want your product, period.*

What we were seeing was that the sampling team members, when faced with an objection to their product, would basically tell the person that they were wrong. The team members led with the negative, which immediately would put the customer on the defensive. So we changed their dialogue just a bit. We taught to them to say this:

Red Bull team member: *Hi, would you like to try a Red Bull?*
Customer: *No, thanks, I heard it was loaded with caffeine.*
Red Bull team member: *Yeah, we get that all the time, did you know Red Bull has about the same amount of caffeine as a regular cup of coffee? You should try it.*

In the first instance, the customer was told that their idea was wrong and that the product is not loaded with caffeine. The customer is probably thinking "Yeah, it is, you are a jackass, and I don't want your product." In the second version we changed the dialogue so that the team member is not leading with a "No," and the dialogue is in fact acknowledging the person's idea. By saying "Yeah, we get that all the time … " the team member has said "yes" to the customer's idea and has not immediately told the customer that what they believe is wrong.

News flash: Nobody likes to be told that they are wrong, *even when they are wrong!* After acknowledging the customer's idea, the team member goes on to educate them about the product "… it has about the same amount as a cup of coffee …" The team member has given the customer information that they previously didn't have and possibly removed a barrier to them trying a Red Bull.

Yes, of course the customer could still say "I don't consume any caffeine" or "I've already had a cup of coffee" or any number of reasons why they don't want to try Red Bull. But maybe that person will consider grabbing a Red Bull the next time they need some energy, or maybe they will even repeat the new fact they learned when someone else says that Red Bull is loaded with caffeine. By acknowledging their initial idea, the team member has a greater chance of keeping that person on their side for a longer amount of time.

Ultimately, if you are only going to interact with the person one time it does not really matter if you say no to them. You will never see them again, so what does it matter? If, though, you are going to have repeated interactions with a person, constantly saying "no" tends to push people away.

We all have had experiences in our lives dealing with a "no" person. What ends up happening is that we learn to go around that person, or over their head, or to another company that is more willing to try to work with us and our ideas.

If you are the "No" person in your organization, you should just be aware how you are probably making at least some people feel. By constantly saying "No" you are losing out on future ideas. When members of the team no longer bring in new ideas, then that is the death of innovation for that organization.

MAYBE

While "No" can stop ideas from moving forward, at least it gives us clarity on what we should or shouldn't do. Making shit up at some point means making decisions, and making decisions means we sometimes have to say "No." From a team creation standpoint what can be at least as bad as "No," and is oftentimes even more problematic, is the "Maybe."

"Maybe" is your wishy-washy friend that can't make a decision. "Maybe" is the weak cousin of "No" that doesn't believe in itself and is unwilling to take decisive action. "Maybe" is even more frustrating for team members to hear than "No" because it leaves them in limbo, not knowing which way to go. Give me a "Yes" or give me a "No," but give me a definitive answer. Without a definitive answer I am stuck waiting and wondering, and that is where negativity is bred.

"Maybe" slows ideas or actions from moving ahead, especially when others are dependent on your decision-making. Just like the concept of "No," the use of "Maybe" is not an absolute. There are times when the use of "maybe" affords us time to consider options. The use of "Maybe" to keep ideas in play as we work through the decision-making process can be a good thing. When used in the positive sense to consider other ways to build on ideas, "Maybe" can be an effective tool to explore new concepts.

When it is used to put off making decisions or to placate people because you don't want to deliver tough information, "Maybe" becomes yet another word that influences ideas in progress in a negative way. If you find yourself constantly saying "Maybe," you need to ask yourself, what is stopping you from making a decision one way or the other? The sooner you answer that question and make a clear decision one way or the other, the sooner you'll be back on the path to making shit up.

YES, AND

So if "No" stops ideas from moving ahead and "Maybe" slows them down, how exactly do we move ideas along to bigger and better concepts? In modern improvisational theater the actors are trained to use the concept of "Yes, and" to quickly move ideas forward and build to completely new and unexpected concepts that each member of the scene can feel ownership of. Many people, when discussing the ideation or creative process think that it is all about saying "Yes." It is often said that all you have to do is say "Yes" to whatever idea that is presented to you. While that is certainly better than saying "No" or "Maybe," just saying "Yes" is not going to get you very far. This is what a scene looks like when someone in it only says "Yes":

Kevin: *Hey, I have two tickets to the Celtics tonight, you want to join me?*
Trevor: *Sure!*
Kevin: *Great, I'll meet you at the Garden at seven.*
Trevor: *Awesome!*
Kevin: *Seems like you're a big fan?*

Trevor:	*Yes!*
Kevin:	*So, then, it should be a pretty good time.*
Trevor:	*Sure!*

While there is no negation going on in this scene, and it is certainly positive and being kept in basic agreement, there still is not a ton that is happening. We are moving the scene along and will eventually end up at the basketball game, but from a creative standpoint it is a one-sided conversation where Kevin is doing all of the work.

More things are being discovered in the scene, but it is relying heavily on the creativity of one person. Trevor isn't stopping the ideas or actions from moving forward, but he isn't contributing much, either. If all we ever do is say "Yes," then we are ceding any control completely to other people.

By only saying "Yes" while not offering any of our own ideas, we are taking a very passive approach to the creative process. At some point, if we are part of a collaborative effort we will be seen as someone who, while not necessarily getting in the way, isn't contributing to the effort or is not pulling enough weight. Look, "Yes" is far better than saying "No" at the beginning of the ideation phase, but only saying "Yes" will often lead to the plateauing of ideas.

It is the *"and"* that kicks the idea in the ass and moves it forward. The "and" leads us to the next action or possibility. The "and" ensures that each participant is offering something new to the scene. Let's take a look at that same scene done with the "Yes, and" technique.

Kevin:	*Hey, I have two tickets to the Celtics tonight. You want to join me?*
Trevor:	*Yes, and we should paint our faces green.*
Kevin:	*Yes, and we will probably get on the Jumbotron.*
Trevor:	*Yes, and we might even get on TV.*
Kevin:	*Yes, and all of our friends will see us and be super jealous.*
Trevor:	*Yes, and we can post pics on Instagram to show how awesome our lives are.*
Kevin:	*Yes, and we'll get tens of thousands of new followers.*
Trevor:	*Yes, and we will become social media superstars and make millions for practically doing nothing.*

Clearly this scene builds in a much faster way than the original basketball scene did. Each time "and" was attached to the "Yes," a new possibility was entered into the scene. By keeping this scene in agreement "and" building off of the idea that was previously stated, the scene quickly built to an unexpected ending. Just saying "Yes" doesn't get us there.

Look, I'm asking you to think metaphorically here for a second, but if our starting point was "I have tickets to the Celtics" and our ending point is becoming "social media superstars," then we would never have gotten there if we did not agree and build upon each other's statements. If Trevor answered "no" when he was asked if he wanted to go to the Celtics game, then the scene would have been dead in the water. Had he said "Maybe," we still may have gotten there, but it would have been slower and more laborious, as Kevin would have had to work to bring Trevor around to his idea.

Does that mean that we go around on stage constantly saying "Yes, and, Yes, and"? Of course not. That would be terrible and artificial and unbearable to watch. Hell, I will even say something that is practically blasphemous in the improv world: "Yes, and" can sometimes be overblown as a concept. If we never explore conflict or disagreement onstage, then we will miss the opportunity to explore opposing points of view or authentic representations of human interaction.

What "Yes, and" does allow for is the ability for people to rapidly get on the same page and build trust with each other. If I know that every time I offer an idea onstage you are going to say "Yes, and" and you know that every time you offer an idea I am going to say "Yes, and," then neither of us have to worry that our ideas are going to be shot down. We don't have to worry that our ideas will be considered stupid or not good enough, and therefore we can fly quickly and create bigger and better ideas that we both feel ownership of.

The essence of "Yes, and" is essentially this: I am truly listening to what it is that you are saying, and then associating off of what I heard and adding on my thoughts and ideas.

Do we actually say "Yes, and" onstage? Rarely. What we do is try to find ways to agree with our scene partners, and then introduce our own perspective on what is happening. "Yes, and" can be said a hundred different ways:

Cool, let's …
Awesome, we should …
Great, now we can …
Sweet, let's go …
Nice, now I'm going to …

The commonality is that the first word agrees in a positive way and then the second part allows the individual to add their own idea. When we advance ideas in this way, with other people or even just with ourselves, we can quickly build to bigger and better ideas that we never knew existed.

Oh, there is one pitfall that I need to make you aware of. While the concept of "Yes, and" can quickly advance ideas and bring people together, as well as build stronger cultures, there is a similar yet ultimately completely different concept that often rears its ugly head in corporate meetings across the globe. That is the concept of "Yes, but." If you have ever been in any kind of business or corporate meeting at any point in your life, then I am sure you are familiar with that insidious, despicable, outright tyrannical concept called "Yes, but." You know, it goes something like this:

Vicky: *I think we should offer surprise discounts to our best customers as a thank you for their continued support.*

Brian: *Yes, but how are we going to identify who our best customers are?*

Vicky: *We can set certain metrics that would identify who our best customers are and look them up in our database.*

Brian: *Yes, but if we do that we maybe make some of our other customers angry.*

Vicky: *Well, we can let those customers know how they can move into the VIP group that allows them to receive these kinds of benefits.*

Brian: *Yes, but we don't even know if the so-called best customers will even value these discounts.*

I hate Brian and so should you. There is nothing easier in the world than pointing out why an idea "might" not work. It takes no skill or imagination to sharpshoot an idea and lay out reasons why a concept could fail.

You most often see this scenario play out in the form of the person who plays the role of "devil's advocate." You know that person? The one who, whenever an idea is presented, raises his or her hand and says (read this in the most whiny and annoying voice that you can imagine), "Well, to play the devil's advocate for a moment here … "

That person makes me want to kill myself. Again, it is simple to shoot down other people's ideas in the beginning stages. Anyone can do it and it takes no talent to do so.

To be clear, I am focusing on the initial exchange of ideas. There is a time in any creative process when the role of "devil's advocate" is very important. Somewhere down the line, tough questions need to be asked, assumptions need to be challenged, and alternative outcomes need to be explored. Yet if an idea is immediately attacked with a "Yes, but" attitude or negative questioning, then we will never discover what might be.

One of the ways that I like to deal with the person who is playing the role of the "Yes, but-er", or "devil's advocate" is to have the person that is criticizing the idea have to immediately offer up an idea of their own or what they think might be a potential solution to the problem that they're pointing out. I ask them to put some intellectual skin in the game.

When someone knows that they are going to have to offer their own ideas and open themselves up to criticism, it is amazing how quickly they back off from ripping everybody else's ideas to shreds. It may sound like semantics, but try having a conversation with someone where are all you do is "Yes, and" each other back and forth for 30 seconds. Then have a new conversation where all you do is "Yes, but" each other back and forth. I guarantee you will find that the "Yes, and" concept is far more collaborative and leads to a multitude of different possibilities, whereas the "Yes, but" conversation will be far more antagonistic and argumentative and lead to fewer new ideas.

When you use "Yes, but" in an argument you are more or less just saying "yes, but no." With "Yes, but," you more often than not are just finding new ways to restate why you are right. Something I like to say to make you remember to try to avoid "Yes, but" in the beginning of the ideation phase is this saying:

"Nothing good comes *out* of the but."

Has this entire book been an elaborate buildup to a juvenile poop joke? Maybe. What I mean by that phrase is that rarely does someone say, upon hearing a new idea "Yes, but, that is awesome!"

There is almost always a negative that comes from the "but." Oddly enough, the concept of "No, but" is an effective way of saying no while still keeping somebody on your side and exploring other opportunities.

Is it the end of the world if you say "Yes, but"? Of course not. Most of us are reasonable human beings and can handle negative words or phrases. I would just suggest that anytime you can change the "but" to an "and," you will have better luck keeping a person or team on your side, which will allow for more positive exchange and buildup of ideas.

"Yes, and" is a tool. It is not the "right" way to create nor is it the only way to create. But it is a proven effective way to discover new ideas and move them along.

How can you practice this? In the next meeting in which you are trying to find a solution to a problem or come up with some new ideas, suggest to the team that for the next 15 minutes everybody uses the "Yes, and" technique of building off of each other's ideas. Even if it is an awful idea that seems insane or you fundamentally hate it.

Commit to "Yes, and-ing" it and seeing where it goes. Do this for 15 minutes and then go back to using all the tools that already work for you and your organization: infighting, accusations, paranoia, and backstabbing. I kid. By treating it as a tool in your ideological toolbox, you now have another way of tackling problems, and one that is simple enough for everyone to understand and attempt right away.

The "Yes, and" technique works in professional relationships, personal relationships, with kids, and even with strangers. Put a little "Yes, and" in your life and I promise you will see significant results in the effectiveness of your communications.

Chapter 10

Small Decisions Add Up

For me, the joy of doing improv comes from the fact that as a performer I am allowed to follow wherever the scene goes without any real expectation to end up anywhere. Once we get the suggestion and the scene is set in motion we have no idea what is going to happen.

The absolute freedom in creating this way is intoxicating. There are very few constraints, and you are not only allowed but encouraged to ride the creative wave wherever it takes you. The unknown, far from being scary, becomes limitless opportunity. When you are improvising on stage, the unknown is alive with possibilities. The sheer pleasure of diving into that pool is exhilarating in the freedom of creativity it allows.

Yet, much like ordering off a menu at The Cheesecake Factory, you may enjoy having hundreds of choices but eventually you have to make a decision.

The ability to make decisions is the catalyst for being able to make shit up. Performing improv requires constant decision-making. Because there is no script explaining stage directions, or director telling the actor where to go or what to say or do, the individual is required to make all of those decisions for themselves.

Indecision on the stage will result in absolutely nothing happening, which will be boring as shit to the audience. The actor is required to make decisions at every step of the way to help move the scene forward.

Improv actors are trained to limit their questions onstage and instead make declarative statements. The reason for this is that strong, clear statements are action oriented. Statements presume action. Statements lead to decisions being made and with each decision made there is a corresponding reaction or results.

Questions, while good for presenting possibilities, slow the action down to a crawl and in some instances can completely stop it. Let me illustrate this concept in a scene.

The scene is a fast-food restaurant. A woman rushes in and quickly glances around. Seeing the person at the counter she quickly steps up to that person and asks:

Kate: *Can I use your bathroom?*
Cashier: *Sorry, bathrooms are only for paying customers.*
Kate: *Okay fine, I'll take an order of fries. Can I have the keys now?*
Cashier: *Would you like to supersize them for 99 cents?*
Kate: *No, thank you! Can I have the keys?*
Cashier: *Will that be cash or credit?*
Kate: *Credit. Keys?*
Cashier: *Would you like to make a donation to support homeless dogs?*

While we can certainly find humor in the scene if we were to keep it going with just questions, the scene would eventually die out and the audience would lose interest. While the game of not giving Kate the keys to the bathroom is at first kind of fun, eventually everybody would become frustrated, including the actor playing Kate. If no declarative statements are stated and no decisions are ever made to take action, then we will just continue to repeat more or less the same idea. In this case the repeating loop is:

"Can I have the keys to the bathroom?"
"No."
"Can I have them now?"
"No."
"Can I have them now?"
"No."

Let's take a look at what the scene might look like if the actors use declarative statements and make decisions.

Kate:	*I need to use your bathroom.*
Cashier:	*Sorry, bathrooms are for paying customers only.*
Kate:	*Look pal, if you don't give me the keys to the bathroom, you're not going to be having any paying customers in this place for the next hour.* The cashier eyes Kate nervously.
Cashier:	(tossing Kate the keys) *Okay, but if my manager finds out I am going to be in big trouble.*
Kate:	(Running to the bathroom and shouting back over her shoulder) *Don't worry, I will vouch for you.* Kate makes all kinds of grunting noises and moaning sounds finishing with a series of high-pitched screams turning into a gratifying exhale. The cashier is reacting with facial expressions to all of the sounds. Kate exits the bathroom and slowly approaches the cashier, casually tossing him the keys.
Kate:	*Thank you so much.* The cashier just nods awkwardly.
Kate:	*I will take one of everything on the menu.*

In this scene no questions were asked and the action was driven forward by declarative statements. Because strong statements were made this lead to decisions being taken by the actors, which advanced the action and the story. Instead of being stuck in a scene that keeps repeating itself, we see the actors go from the interaction at the counter to the bathroom, where we hear all kinds of sounds, then back to the counter where Kate orders one of everything on the menu. This is a far more interesting scene to both be a part of as well as watch.

Statements and decisions drive the creative process outside of improv as well. If we are going to make shit up we have to become comfortable with making decisions. Maybe in your life you are not in a position to constantly make big or important decisions. No matter. Like everything else we have explored in this book, the way to get better at doing anything is to start small.

Making regular small decisions is far more practical then making big ones. Realistically, the need to make "big decisions" is much more rare than the need to make the little ones. It is the little ones that steadily drive the action forward toward whatever goal we have set for ourselves.

The beauty of making small decisions again and again is that the consequences of these decisions tends to be less, so therefore we do not perceive these kinds of decisions as quite as stressful as having to make big or life-altering ones. The other benefit you get is the confidence gained from repetition. The more decisions you make, the more reps you get, the more confident you get at making decisions. Hey, if you haven't figured it out by now then you are definitely not paying attention. It is all about the reps. The more reps you do at anything, the better you will get at it. Making decisions is no exception.

Making statements and practicing small decision-making is something you can do every day in your own personal life. Some of this may sound like semantics, but take a look at the subtle difference when you change a basic question into a statement:

Dude #1: *You want to grab a smoothie?*
Dude #2: *Maybe.*

Now take a look with the dialogue changed to statements.

Dude #1: *Let's grab a smoothie.*
Dude #2: *Okay.*

By making something a statement instead of a question, you are more likely to steer the conversation or the action toward your own ends. On a very basic level it is just harder for people to deny a statement. Questions, particularly closed ones, can elicit a yes or no response. To make shit happen we need to get more yeses than no's, so therefore we need to drive our ideas forward whenever possible with strong confident statements.

Am I saying we should never ask questions? Of course not. Open-ended questions, questions of possibility, the "What if" or "How might we" or "Why does" type of question helps us discover new information. Open-ended questions are excellent tools in the ideation phase of the creative process. Questions help us with clarity on things we don't understand or that might be confusing. Once you get to the "making shit happen" phase, though, they can slow the decision-making process down to a crawl.

So a very simple way to practice this technique is to try to turn simple questions into declarative statements. You can use this technique on coworkers, your spouse, your kids, your boss, or whomever. If you are not used to being assertive, these kinds of statements may initially feel a bit aggressive. But what you'll find is that the statements themselves will boost your confidence and the people around you, subconsciously or not, will begin to perceive you as more competent.

While statements drive the action forward, it is the ability to make a decision that sets the agenda as to where the action or idea goes to next. By focusing on making small decisions about things that are within our control we then keep the action going and continue to move toward our end goal. It keeps us focused on what is in front of us and what we can actually get done and helps us worry less about the "Big Hairy Scary Picture."

Making small decisions gives us confidence: It keeps us focused on controlling the things that we can control and not worrying so much about the things we can't.

What does making a bunch of small decisions look like? It might look something like this:

End goal: Open an improv theater

Decision #1	Decide what neighborhoods would be good for an improv theater (the North End).
Decision #2	Decide to walk around that neighborhood looking for spaces.
Decision #3	Decide to call the real estate number on the For Rent sign of the theater door.
Decision #4	Decide to get a tour of the theater.
Decision #5	Decide to find out what the rent is.
Decision #6	Decide to see if we are eligible for a small business loan (we are).
Decision #7	Decide to accept the small business loan.
Decision #8	Decide to sign the lease.

If you look at all of the decisions, it wasn't until number 7 that any of them had any major consequences. Each decision was small and was mostly within our control. If we wanted to look at neighborhoods we could. If we wanted to look for spaces we could. It was within our power to call the real estate agent to set up the tour and find out what the rent was. Each of those decisions was within our power and making them led us to the next logical step in the story.

The power of small decisions is that individually they hold very little risk, but taken collectively they propel us toward our final destination. Small decisions consistently ensure that we continue to make gains that lead us to our end goal. It is easy to become intimidated by looking at a huge task before us. Breaking it down into small manageable parts makes whatever we are working on feel like it is much more doable.

In improv the actors on stage are constantly making small decisions. Once the actors get the suggestion from the audience they don't worry about what the entire scene is going to look like, they just begin with the small decisions that they need to make that are right before them. Where am I, who am I?

Once that basic information is established, then they listen to their scene partner and make small decisions based on what they hear. If they find that they are on a sailboat, an actor may decide to hoist a sail. They do not need to worry about where the sailboat is going or what can happen to the sailboat or why they are even on the sailboat. They just need to take that one action, in this instance raising the sail. Their scene partner then makes a decision for themselves. Maybe they decide to scan the horizon with binoculars. They then decide what they see. Maybe they are being approached by a party boat. One of the actors decides to make contact with the party ship by calling out to them. An actor offstage decides to respond. An actor on the sailboat decides to throw them a line and pull them in. One of the actors on the party boat decides to tie the line off. The other actor on the party boat decides to step onto the sailboat with a cooler full of booze. The actors on the sailboat proceed to chug all the booze and get drunk. The actors on the party boat decide to tie up the actors on the sailboat and steal all of their stuff, because they are party boat pirates.

Clearly there would be dialogue throughout the scene (although you could probably do this entire scene with no dialogue and communicate almost everything through physical actions), but that dialogue either justifies a decision or leads to another.

Each small decision builds upon the last one leading to a full scene that nobody knew was going to happen. The actors are never worried about what the final outcome of the scene would be because they are focused on being in the moment, listening to what is being said, and then continuing to make a series of small decisions.

Decision-making can be practiced. Here are a couple of easy ways to practice decision-making on a small scale:

The next time you go to a restaurant read through the menu once. Immediately decide what you're going to order, then close the menu and put it down.

When you are at the bar, look at your beer choices once, and then pick one.

When you get dressed in the morning (or whenever you get dressed – comedy people are typically not morning people so it is more like the afternoon for us), see how fast you can pick everything out. Try not to overthink it. Just grab your clothes as fast you can and get dressed.

Whenever somebody asks you a basic question, something like "Where do you want to go to dinner?" or "What movie do you want to watch?" immediately answer with one suggestion.

Since each of the examples above are low-risk decisions, there is no harm in trying to make them as fast as you can. So what if you end up with an IPA when you really would have preferred a stout, had you taken more time to think about it? We are practicing fast thinking and decision-making, not considered thinking in decision-making.

What you will eventually find is that you can start to make simple decisions much faster without the need to endlessly consider your options and with far less anxiety. You will also stop annoying the crap out of your friend at the bar who just wants you to pick a beer and get on with it.

And that is a key component of making shit up. Make a decision and get on with it.

Chapter 11

The Cult Factor

In general, people follow passion and energy, not ideas. Don't believe me? Then just take a look at cults. Cults are populated by devoted followers who enthusiastically and staunchly believe in and defend the theories and principles that the cult preaches. They are typically led by a single charismatic leader who, through seemingly sheer animal magnetism, entrances a community of followers to such a degree that the leader's words and beliefs are accepted as gospel.

Now, here is the thing. More often than not those ideas are batshit crazy. From believing aliens are going to come down and take them away on a certain date, or that by the force of group thought people can make themselves invisible, to far more dangerous and sinister ideas, the concepts that cults often follow seem absolutely ludicrous to someone from the outside looking in. So why do perfectly reasonable and intelligent people end up falling under the spell of these shamans?

It ain't the Kool-Aid. It is the fact that humans respond to and follow energy and passion. Humans are drawn to other humans who create energy and stimulate emotions. We are tribal creatures and are genetically programmed to come together in groups for protection. Most other animals were faster and stronger and thicker-skinned than our ancient selves, so that meant that they could kill us far more easily than we could kill them.

The only thing we had going for us was our abnormally big brain and our ability to procreate and live together in relatively larger numbers. Our brains allowed us to devise more clever ways to both kill the other animals as well as not get killed by them. The fact that we lived in larger groups gave us strength in numbers and also allowed for the tribe to survive, even if a couple of us got picked off by the occasional lion or grizzly bear.

The tribal members, believing death was around every corner, and it was, needed someone to say, "Hey, man, we got this." If the leader said it loud enough and with enough passion, the rest of the tribe would be like "Hey, maybe we do got this," and they would follow the leader until he got himself killed or she got too many other people killed. Afterwards they would all come together and complain about what an idiot the leader had been.

The cycle would repeat itself again and again all the way up until modern times where we have seen a split in the Homo sapien line where a new species, Homo entrepreneurus, identified by the curious trait of believing they can do anything and the ability to somehow get others to believe so, as well.

I know what a bunch of you are thinking right now. Charisma ain't my jam. I am never going to be able to get all Chris Farley "Man who lives in a van down by the river" (younger people, please do yourself a favor and look this up on YouTube) for anyone or anything. You might be saying to yourself *I am quiet, I am an introvert, I don't like to draw attention to myself, talking in front of a crowd makes me want to throw up,* or any other number of justifications as to why you could never be that kind of leader.

All of these things may be entirely true. What you should also know is that anyone, regardless of their personality type, can tap into passion and energy and increase their charisma.

Charisma, like creativity, is often thought of as some mysterious gift that only the specially anointed have been given. There is the common belief that when it comes to the ability to command a room by force of personality, you either got it or you don't.

I won't blow smoke up your butt and deny that this skill doesn't come more easily to some anymore than math or languages or playing the guitar comes to others. We are not all wired the same, thank God. So clearly some will pick up certain skills and abilities faster than others. Yet just like math or languages or playing an instrument the ability to manufacture energy and passion can be learned.

You may be thinking to yourself "I don't need people to follow me. I'm not looking to be a cult leader. I just have some ideas that I want to move forward. I can do that without being high energy or crazy passionate."

You are right. You can. It will also be that much harder to have people pay attention to your ideas. If there is no passion or emotion behind your ideas it makes it much more difficult for people to lock in to what you're talking about. There is a very simple reason for this; if there is no passion or energy behind your ideas, they come off as very monotone.

The brain is wired to eventually tune out a constant dull sound that never changes. If you are in a room and quietly observe your surroundings, you will invariably begin to notice certain constant sounds that you had ignored before. The humming of a refrigerator. The buzz in the overhead lights. The whooshing of an air conditioner. You hadn't noticed them before because those sounds are monotonous and steady, and your brain quickly adjusted to them and decided they did not mean much, so you didn't have to really pay any attention to them.

It is the same thing with ideas and the ability to make shit up and move things forward. If you can't project a certain level of passion around your idea when you are talking about it, getting others to execute it, or even executing it yourself, it will become that much harder.

So how does someone become more charismatic and energetic? Is it as simple as jumping up and down on a trampoline, standing in your power pose, or shouting at the top of your lungs "I am awesome!"? Actually, it can be. Those kinds of things work because you are changing your physical and/or emotional state. You are getting your heart rate up, which gets the blood and oxygen flowing and releases endorphins to the brain.

If you are comfortable with doing these things or are in an environment that allows for this to happen, then by all means give them a try. The reality for many of us is that we don't have a trampoline readily available to us at the office, or perhaps shouting "I am awesome!" at the top of our lungs will scare the shit out of our coworkers and most likely land us in Carol from HR's office.

There are other more practical and attainable ways to work on your ability to increase your passion and energy. Let's look at energy first. What I mean by energy is the general mood or feelings you outwardly project. We all know that person who walks into the room and immediately brings everybody down. They are not even trying, yet just by being themselves they immediately bum everybody out. They don't even need to say anything, it is just in the way they carry themselves. Typically it is a low-energy person who moves extremely slow, has bad posture, and often exhales or sighs before they speak. When they do speak they tend to use words or images that gravitate toward the negative. They habitually point out what is wrong or likely to go wrong as well as highlight the challenges or obstacles that will be faced in doing something. They rarely get excited by other people's ideas, often speak in a low monotone.

This person is an energy vampire and you can't help but not want to be around them. It doesn't matter if they are intelligent, or nice or that they may have great ideas. When exposed to these kinds of people for any length of time, the majority of people will not want to consistently engage with them.

Contrast that with their opposite counterpart. The person who walks into the room and it immediately lights up. The person who everybody wants to greet and say hello to. The individual who seems to fill whatever space they are in. This person is often characterized by having a physical sense of energy. The move just a bit faster than everyone else. They stand erect and often have an open, shoulders-back posture. They make eye contact as they speak, being sure to use a clear volume. They smile more, laugh more easily, and tend to use more positive words and exclamations. When they are talking they use inflection in their sentences and vary their pace and tone. You don't necessarily have to like them and they may not be particularly nice, but how they present themselves and their ideas tends to grab and hold the listener's attention sooner and longer than the person who is an energy vampire.

Energy can be managed and manipulated in fairly easy ways. We all have a baseline energy that we default to. The speed at which we move during the normal course of the day is what I would call our general baseline energy. A simple way of increasing this energy is by consciously moving just a bit faster than we normally do.

For instance, if I am walking down the hall at my normal unthinking pace, I can easily decide to speed up and move just a bit quicker. This will have the natural result of slightly increasing my heart rate and my oxygen intake as well as send slightly different signals to my brain. Others that are around me will subconsciously pick up on the increased energy that I am exerting and respond in kind.

I am not advocating that you all of a sudden run around like you just drank a case of Red Bull (full disclosure: Red Bull is a client of ours, and I highly recommend you drink as much Red Bull as you can), as manic energy makes people nervous and can cause them to lose confidence in you.

What I am suggesting is that you slightly increase your pace to a level that you can maintain over a length of time. While your physical fitness level will determine to a degree how fast you can move, there is almost always a way to exert just a bit more energy in your day-to-day movements.

The same concept holds true with how you speak. Many of us find ourselves in an environment where, without even meaning to do so, we begin to sound alike. I believe there is something in our brain that makes us all want to conform in sound and style of speech. Again, I'm sure it is a defense mechanism that tries to keep from being singled out in a group, which would then open us up to suspicion and ridicule and, eventually, burning at the stake.

We can apply the same techniques to our speech patterns. The first and easiest exercise is to speak louder. I know this must seem like an incredibly trite insight, but I can assure you this, if you consider yourself quiet or shy or an introvert, just increasing your volume a small amount will return great dividends in terms of the energy you exude.

Again, this is not about being loud and obnoxious. Loud and obnoxious people need to tone it the F down. But for those of you who feel that creating energy is a struggle, then the simple act of speaking louder grabs and holds others' attention in a way very low volume can't.

While energy is often a physical manifestation, it can be truly manipulated through the use of passion. Passion can be manufactured; hell, more often than not it needs to be manufactured. Maybe you have a job and every single day you get up in morning and you just can't wait to get your day started and get into the office and live your best life. I applaud and envy you.

While that may be something that I aspire to, the reality is that there are plenty of days I need to artificially create that passion. Much like creating energy for ourselves, creating passion can be done in a similar way. Passion is both delivered and received speech. Slightly changing *how* we speak can go a long way toward changing how our words are received. Let's take a look at one of the most common places people actually see your passion, or a lack thereof. Public speaking.

I often get asked to coach executives on how to be better public speakers. Fear of public speaking is common and afflicts a huge swath of humanity, from CEOs to teenagers giving an oral presentation on the American Revolution. In a *Washington Post* survey, the fear of public speaking was the number 1 fear, outclassing such favorites as heights, snakes, drowning, zombies, and clowns.

In an intense immersive training program that I have been codesigning with former Special Forces operators, called Series 18, the activity that caused the most anxiety for the participants was not being hooded and interrogated, not escaping in handcuffs from a blackened room, not rappelling off a cliff, or firing AK-47s. Across the board, the activity that scared everybody the most was the improv exercise. The fear of looking and sounding stupid in front of other people is so deeply ingrained in the human psyche that people feel more comfortable potentially falling off a cliff and dying then looking like a jackass in front of their peers.

By being on stage and speaking to audiences for the last 20 years, I have developed the ability to communicate my thoughts to large groups of people, so it only makes sense that others who want to get better at public speaking might ask me to show them some tricks and techniques. During a break during one of the team trainings I was facilitating for a very large financial institution, one of the executives pulled me aside and asked me if I could give him some tips on improving the presentation that he was scheduled to deliver the next day.

I'm sure he was expecting some deep insights in commanding the stage and mesmerizing the audience through theatrical flair. I looked at him and said one word: *"Inflect."*

"That's it?" he responded, incredulous. Yeah, that's it. Inflect. If I could give one piece of advice that will immediately make any speech better, it is to inflect different words when you talk. I don't *care* which ones you pick to INFLECT. They can be NOUNS or *they can BE* verbs or any other DAMN word you *choose*. But by simply inflecting different words when you talk you will automatically be better than 90 percent of the speakers who drone on and on, never once altering how they emphasize words.

I could tell this guy was skeptical and wasn't overly impressed with my simplistic answer. So when we came back as a group from break, I decided it was a good opportunity to demonstrate this technique, not only for him but the rest of the group. I let everybody know the question that I received and the answer I gave. I then looked around the room for some kind of signage. On the wall there was a sign that gave instructions on what to do in case of emergency. It read something like this:

> In case of an emergency please exit through the fire doors that can be found at either end of the room. Fire extinguishers are placed in the front and back of the auditorium. Please exit in an orderly fashion and assembled in the designated team area.

First I read the instructions in your typical corporate/10th-grade oral report monotone. Then I read it again like this (caps indicate inflection):

> In case of an EMERGENCY please exit through the FIRE Doors that can be FOUND at EITHER end of the room. Fire EXTINGUISHERS are placed in the front AND back of the auditorium. PLEASE exit in an ORDERLY fashion and ASSEMBLE in the DESIGNATED team area.

Through the simple act of inflecting, adding emphasis to various words to break up the monotonous pattern, I took a simple instructional sign and gave it some life and passion. It perfectly illustrated the point that just by emphasizing certain words, you break up the auditory patterns, and this helps the listener stay engaged and not drift off into another world.

While this certainly works in any kind of speech for public presentation, simply adding inflection to your day-to-day speech pattern will help you manufacture a bit of passion in how you sound to others. Take a look at these two lines of dialogue:

Hello Patty, How are you today?
Hello PATTY, how are YOU today?

Same sentence, But the second one read with inflection on PATTY and YOU totally changes the energy and passion of that sentence. I'm not advising you to be insane and over-the-top, but by simply adding a little bit of volume and inflection in how you speak, you will start to come off as a more effective communicator.

Then start adding in a few positive exclamatory words, and you will begin to sound far more passionate than you probably feel. Compare these two lines of dialogue:

I got an Italian sub. It was pretty good.
I got a TREMENDOUS Italian sub. It was FANTASTIC!

Look, I can regale you with all kinds communication theory and intricate improv exercises that will allow you to tap into your inner truth and bring forth your authentic self in such a way that those around you cannot deny your divine being. Or, I can show you a couple of practical, easily executable techniques that can be practiced and applied in real life scenarios. So that is what I've done.

By increasing our energy and passion in how we communicate, we can't help but draw people toward us. And while that may not be the end goal, if we are looking to move ideas ahead, at some point it almost always requires buy-in from someone else: the boss, the team, your spouse, your kids, or your friends.

Most important, your energy and passion is something you alone have control over. You do not have to wait for someone else to give you permission to raise your energy and passion. When you do, you will find that invariably more positive things will be set into motion in your life.

Chapter 12

Be Patiently Impatient

I'm the most patiently impatient person I know. On the one hand, I believe in making shit happen as soon as possible. Cut out the crap that wastes time or doesn't make sense to do. Cut corners as long as you are not hurting anyone physically, emotionally, or financially. If you ask for permission from someone else you are going to wait a long time to do what you want to do.

On the other hand, I can play the long game. Yes, I'm trying to make shit happen now, but I also have my eye on a much longer play down the road. I can wait out the idiots, the bureaucrats, the haters, and the cowards.

What I lack in talent, and it's a lot, I make up for in the ability to keep coming back again and again and again. I can accept short-term setbacks because my goal is not immediate gratification but to be standing there at the end, however long it takes.

To both stay in the game and move it along, you need to be patient and impatient. If all you are is constantly impatient, you will oftentimes become frustrated at the perceived lack of progress. Everything can seem like it is taking an excruciatingly long time to move forward.

This often leads to discouragement and ultimately giving up on whatever it is you are pursuing. Chronic impatience can lead to a person starting a bunch of different projects but never completing anything. If you are in a leadership position, constant impatience can dramatically increase the stress and anxiety of your subordinates.

If you are patient to the point of accepting everyone else's timelines, you are going to waiting forever, sister. If you never force the issue, state your desires, or ask for what you want, you are going to be sitting at that cubicle for a long, lonely time.

Nobody is going to be running up to you breathlessly asking for your brilliant idea or opinion. You will be home on Friday night writing a book that no one has asked for (wait a second, that's what I'm doing right now). Life moves by incredibly fast. While patience may be a virtue, it can also be a sin in regards to making shit up and moving things along.

I have found that being impatient in regards to taking action is extremely powerful. Relentlessly push along the things that you tangibly can. There is always something you can do today for any project or idea you are working on, no matter how big or small. Sure, you will annoy certain people. They will tell you to slow down, ease up a little. As a general rule I tend to never listen to anybody who tells me that. Not saying they are wrong, I just figure I will push forward regardless and deal with the results. That is what I am going for, results. Not perfection. Not even near perfection, but tangible results that I can evaluate and then build on. The imperfect results are always better then the near-perfect idea that never gets implemented.

Being extremely patient on the long-term goal or outcome has probably been the main reason for any sustained success I have ever had. When everyone else quits or dies, if you are still there lurching along like a *Walking Dead* zombie, you have taken the lead.

This skill is absolutely learned. As a kid and a young adult I was all impatience and no finish. I never truly learned the ability to stick with much of anything and see it through to the end, unless I enjoyed it (football, school play). I was very immature and underdeveloped in the area of fulfilling commitments.

The upside of this was that I honed my skills at cutting corners, or as they are fashionably referred to today, "life hacks" (euphemism for cheating). The downside was I made things much harder for myself than they probably should have been. By not developing the ability to see things through to the finish in my early years, I ended up failing at things I really had no reason to fail at. I would have to repeat classes or tasks that I easily could have completed the first time around if I only had the wherewithal to see it through to the end.

To this day I still find it hard to consistently practice the patience part of the game. What I find helpful in sticking with whatever project or idea I'm working on is to make sure that I acknowledge the little successes along the way. I am not someone who creates from a negative place. Beating myself up has never been a particularly effective motivation.

Now, I'm not averse to the periodic "Whoa is me" moments, and have been known to say to myself "Stop being such a (unflattering word) and get your ass going," but overall I have found that positively acknowledging the small things has given me the confidence to keep moving forward. The trick is to celebrate the seemingly insignificant stuff and turn it into a series of wins. You want to make 10 phone calls a day to set up meetings about your idea? Start with one call and acknowledge that you took a step in the direction of your final destination. That then gives you the confidence to make three calls, then five, then 10.

You get the picture. Since it will always be a long time before you get to celebrate the final product, be it a show or business or marriage, finding ways to positively recognize the progress you are making becomes very helpful in sustaining the patience that the longevity of creating something new requires.

How can you practice being both productively patient and impatient? Let's look at practicing impatience first. Take a look at something in your life where you are not getting the results that you want. It might be something as common as getting into shape. Quickly list some of the things that are holding you back. Maybe you think you don't have the time or you can't afford a gym membership or you're overwhelmed by the P90X/Gladiator/ Goddess/Insanity/whatever-the-hell workout you have been reading about.

Some people associate impatience with being annoyed. I associate it with taking action. So in this case what actions can be taken immediately? Don't have the time to exercise? Set your alarm one hour earlier. Don't think about it. Don't question it. Just do it right now. That took you all of 10 seconds. Can't afford a gym membership or don't know what exercises to do? When that alarm goes off, force yourself out of bed and go for a walk. That's it. By embracing your impatience, you have forced the issue to start exercising.

If you continue to be impatient and take these actions, you can start adding in jogging or push-ups or planks. Most of us lack a certain amount of motivation. Trying to use the big picture to motivate ourselves can be intimidating. Committing to something small, like setting your alarm, isn't scary and can be done immediately.

I've always found that when I do something immediately, it begins to create momentum that helps propel me toward my goal. Being impatient helps create the motivation I need to do shit.

So how can we practice patience? There are great philosophers and far deeper thinkers than me that can set you on the path of self-awareness and enlightenment. For me, it is as simple as showing up, again and again. Patience is about showing up and being there in the moment again and again without any major expectations of results.

This is actually the way I have built Improv Asylum. I have often been asked what was the secret of Improv Asylum's success? While I would love to say that it is a direct result of my creative genius, unfathomable talent, and singular vision to bring something extraordinary to life, that would be one crock of hot garbage. The single most important thing we ever did at Improv Asylum was to decide to open the doors, turn on the lights, and do shows. Night after night. That's it. Sorry everybody, if you were hoping for some mind-blowing truth, I got nothing for you.

Quite frankly, the genius lay in the decision to make sure that the doors were open and shows were going on every night of every weekend. It had been our experience at other theaters that they operate with some kind of arbitrary number for audience attendance that must to be met, or the show will be canceled. For example, if they have 10 or more people in the audience, the show will go on, and if the audience is below 10, the show is canceled and the audience is sent home. I have always considered this to be the height of stupidity.

Let's take a look of this from a pragmatic point of view. If the breaking point for doing a show is having 10 people in the audience, then it certainly can't be about money. I mean, it is not like you are in the red at 9 people in the audience, but in the black at 11. Whether the number is 9 or 11 *you are in the red*! So if you are losing money either way, why wouldn't you just do the show for the nine people that came to see it?

The other, more damaging, thing is that if you cancel that show those 9 people who came all the way down to the theater to see your nonsense are going to be annoyed, if not outright pissed, and most likely will never be coming back to another show. On the other hand, if you go out on that stage and do your damnedest to make a great show happen for those nine people, at least some of them are going to be appreciative, and not only will they come back, but they will bring more people with them.

We had made the decision at the very beginning at Improv Asylum that we would never cancel shows because of the audience size. If five people were there we would do a show. If there were two people we would do the show. If there was one person who is willing to watch the show then we would put on a performance just for them (we actually did that). If nobody was there, then we would run through the show anyway, because we always need the practice.

This attitude has had a powerful effect on both our audiences and also our casts. In the early days those small audiences were incredibly appreciative of the fact that we would do a show for them. While performing for small audiences can at first feel awkward, when they see that you are truly trying to do good work just for them, they tend to get behind you.

What ended up happening was that as Improv Asylum became more and more successful, those people who had come to early shows when there were only 5 or 10 people in the audience would come up to us and almost brag that they were here before we became popular, and they were always so thrilled to now be a part of a sold-out show.

They felt like they had something to do with our success, and they most certainly did. Had we sent those people away because of some artificial attendance number, we would have been losing advocates who ended up spreading the word and giving us marketing far more valuable than any ad could buy. Because we were there, night after night, people didn't have to guess whether the show was happening or not. They always knew that the show was on even if it was a very personal performance.

What it did for the casts was that it removed the uncertainty as to whether or not shows were going to happen. Uncertainty will always lead to anxiety and stress. Since the cast knew in no uncertain terms that we were always going to do a show, that was one less thing they would have to worry about.

The consistency of always showing up and always doing the show allowed for the gradual buildup to success. Was it patience? Sure. But it was active patience in the sense that we were there, showing up every time, without any major expectations for results.

What is something you can keep showing up to without worrying about or overly measuring the results? Is it a class of some sort? Maybe it's painting and you just keep showing up and you just keep painting without ever giving a second thought as to how "good" your painting is. If you keep showing up again and again and again, you will get better.

It is just reps. Everything in life is reps. And if you have the patience to keep showing up and putting in the reps, you will undoubtedly improve at whatever it is you are doing.

Chapter 13

Pain Tolerance

What is your pain tolerance? What is your pain tolerance for missing out on social events? From hanging out with your friends? From your girlfriend or boyfriend being mad at you because you aren't spending enough time with them? From your parents or your spouse or other loved ones wondering when you're going to give up this crazy pipe dream and do something productive with your life? For criticism, for doubt? For embarrassment and hurt egos? How much pain can you deal with – emotional psychological spiritual, and sometimes even physical? That was a real bummer of a paragraph, huh?

I believe that pain tolerance or lack thereof directly correlates to success or failure in the long run in any endeavor we decide to embark upon. Everybody has ideas. Tons and tons of people hustle and work hard. You can always be sure that there are more talented, smarter, more connected, better-capitalized people than you.

One of the key things that sets me apart from others is my tolerance for pain. As you try to do something original or innovative, you are going to be faced with all of the scenarios that I mentioned above. What I have seen over the course of my career is that the people who could push through these painful situations have been the ones who more often than not come out on the other side and find success.

This is not just metaphorical pain that I am talking about. This is pain that you really feel. When your boyfriend or girlfriend is mad at you because you are doing yet another series of shows on the weekend and you are missing another night out with their friends or a special event, you feel a pain that is real.

When someone you love or respect or care about doubts what you are doing or thinks you are making mistake, you feel that loss of trust just as powerfully as any physical hurt. When you see all your peers finding a certain amount of success and security, marching on in their own careers while you are still stuck at the start in a world where success is not guaranteed, and is even unlikely, you will feel it like a punch in the gut.

Nobody would blame you if you quit or gave up, and many will probably encourage you to do so.

I would love to sit here and tell you that pursuing your own path is nothing but pure pleasure and a sure way to achieve personal and professional bliss. That, of course, would be utter bullshit. And I am not here to bullshit you. There are many other wonderful professionals you can turn to if that is what you are looking for.

Is charting your own path fulfilling and gratifying in a way that may be difficult to achieve working for the man? Oftentimes, yes. Can it be exciting and mentally and emotionally stimulating to a degree that is tough to find in a safe and ordinary world? Absolutely. Could I or would I choose any other approach? 100 percent no.

Setting an original course cannot happen without a certain amount of pain, Self-doubt and nausea-inducing anxiety. The execution phase of making shit up for a living is far more difficult than the ideation phase. To be blunt, it ain't for everybody.

Then again, pain is all relative. What is painful for me might not cause you any trouble, and vice versus. It is all in the tolerance. The more you can withstand the discomforts that come along with doing your own thing, the further along down the road you will get. Just like with alcohol, you can build up your tolerance to this kind of pain.

One way is by rethinking what pain means. Most of us associated pain with negativity. Pain is something to be avoided at all cost. But what if we change our perspective on what is painful and what it means?

One of the most common comments I get from people when they learn what I do is "Man, what you do is so hard." Another common refrain is "Making it in show biz is really tough." Yeah, I guess. I mean, yes, it certainly is. But ultimately, what isn't?

Seems to me like going to law school is super tough, and med school, holy shitballs, that is *hard*. And I cannot think of too many things harder than working on the auto factory line (my mom) or driving trucks (my dad). Now *that* is hard. *That* is working for a living.

What is perceived as hard or difficult is all relative. For me, the idea of having to get up every morning and be at the same place at 8:30 a.m. and not be able to leave until 5:00 p.m., well, that seems almost impossibly difficult. And yet others look at performers and say that there is no way they could ever go on stage in front of a bunch of strangers and try to make them laugh, without a script, no less!

Yet there is something pleasurable in "hard." It is what gives the thing value. It is what makes us feel like we are accomplishing something or doing something worthwhile. When we can start to change what we perceive to be "hard" and actually connect good feelings to that sensation then we start to look at that endeavor in a whole new light. We look forward to the challenges that the task or the day presents. No longer is the idea of something being "hard" a negative or a deterrent form doing something. The whole idea that something is "hard" is actually a motivating factor for doing it.

It is the same idea with pain. If we remind ourselves that the pain we are experiencing in the immediate moment or in the short term is a symptom of the growth we are experiencing, then it gives us reason to push through it.

We all understand the pain we feel when we first begin to work out. We know that it is there because we are stretching and strengthening our muscles. As we go through the inevitable difficulties that come with doing something out of the ordinary, we need to remember that the pain we are experiencing in the moment is not permanent and will make us stronger and more resilient down the line.

Without being a masochist or a martyr, if we can associate some of that pain we are experiencing with pleasure, kind of an S-and-M thing for the mind, the pain we are feeling no longer has such an intense negative connotation.

What is something that you have always wanted to do, but thought that was too hard or seemed like it would be too painful? What if you changed that thought and instead said, "I'm going to do it exactly because it seems hard or difficult"?

If we wait for everything to be easy before we try to do it, then we probably will be waiting forever. Don't wait for the easy thing. Look for something hard to do and attack it with enthusiasm and passion. When we do that, we redefine what it means for something to be "hard." The pain that comes with it is just a symptom of our own resilience growing, and confirmation that we are pushing outside of our own comfort zone into new and exciting territory.

I will give you a personal example from my own experience. As an actor in a cast at Improv Asylum you are required to be able to do more than just make the audience laugh. You have to write, be able to perform written material, master the art of improvisation, and be able to technically work with your cast mates. Sometimes you have to dance and you almost always have to sing.

As a performer I generally did not have that much difficulty with everything listed above, except for one thing. And that thing was singing. I have been funny in one way shape or form since I was a kid, so in the grand scheme of things I've never been overly worried about that aspect of the job. The writing process is always enjoyable to me, so I have been able to pick up that fairly quickly. I had done plays in high school and college and hundreds of TV commercials, so I've always felt comfortable working with the written word. Singing? Not so much.

Holding notes, hearing notes, finding the pitch, following the melody, all those things were very foreign to me. I learned early on that singing was not my forte and it never would be. That was more than okay because I wasn't looking to become a star of musical comedies. The problem arose when I began to find myself getting cast in comedy troupes.

Turns out, a lot of people in comedy troupes have legit theater backgrounds and training, and many of them love to do musical comedy. So much so that they were always creating some kind of parody song or group number or improvised musical piece. Being part of the ensemble, I was expected to contribute like anybody else. Problem was, I kind of sucked at it. The other actors are usually quite nice about it, but you know when you are the weak link in something. People's voices change when they talk to the weak link. It becomes softer, a higher pitch, slower and sadder. They don't mean to, but they begin to talk to you like a dunce. When it came to singing, I was a dunce.

I had a choice to make. I could either accept the pitying encouragements of my castmates, all the while knowing that they were cringing every time I open my mouth in a song, or I could try to tackle things on my own and try to get better.

So that is what I did. Whenever I was in a show that featured some kind of singing, I made sure to enroll myself in private vocal lessons. Twice a week for 30 minutes or so I would work with someone who would take me through the "me me me's, la la la la's" and the "tip of the tongue on the top of the teeth" exercises.

At first these lessons were excruciating. I could see it on my instructor's face whenever I had to sing something. He was encouraging, but I'm not an idiot. I could also hear myself. Yet in another instance, proving that consistent dogged persistence at something will result in some kind of improvement, I was able to get myself to be able to at least reasonably blend with the rest of the cast on the group numbers. Now, I never had a solo, nor did I want or deserve one.

That was, up until that point where I decided that I should be able to at least sing one thing on my own at some point in my life. I needed to face this fear to prove to myself that I could in fact do it. I knew it was going to be both hard and painful. But I also knew that the confidence I would get from doing something that I always told myself I couldn't do would be invaluable. So I signed up for a far more intensive singing course at a local university in Boston.

Beyond just private lessons, this class ended with each student singing a solo piece to live audience in a theater on campus. When that fateful evening came I stood on the stage all by my lonesome and sang a solo number from *Les Misérables*. The Hollywood version of this story ends with the audience rising to their feet amidst thunderous applause an intermittent shouts of "Bravo!" and "Encore!" Alas, that was not to be. My performance was mediocre at best and was met with the polite indifference of people who are forced to sit through uninspired performances from amateur singers.

When I came off that stage I felt like a badass! I just sang a song in front of hundreds of people by myself, something that in a million years I thought I would never do. I had faced down a fear and proved to myself that I could push through the pain of this very personal obstacle and accomplish a goal that I had always thought to be impossible.

Did I become a great singer? No. A good one? Not even. What I no longer had was the fear of musical numbers. The worry and anxiety that came with having to perform those pieces were gone. The hard work and the pain made me stronger and more confident, and that allowed me to be a stronger and more confident performer when it came to singing songs like "Jesus Christ, Superstore," "Kindergarten Pressure," or "Bingo with Nana." In case you had forgotten, we aren't performing things like Les Misérables in our stinky basement theaters. We make stupid shit up for a living

How can you practice this? Pick something you have always wanted to try but thought would be too hard or too painful to do. Maybe it is learning a new language or playing an instrument. Maybe it is singing. Sign up for a class and see it through. Don't focus on or particularly care about the end results. The goal isn't to be amazingly awesome at whatever it is you are learning. The goal is to do something hard and push through the pain to prove to yourself that you can achieve a goal that is difficult.

By first experiencing this when the results are ultimately inconsequential (at the end of the day, who really gives a shit if you become proficient at the ukulele), you start to develop a tolerance to pain and an ability to push on through when things become hard, because you know how good it will feel when you reach your goal.

Chapter 14

Luck Is Like a Train

You can't get hit by luck if you don't stand in front of it. I listen to many people comment about how lucky I am, or how lucky others have been. How it is better to be lucky than good, that some people just have all the luck.

While there is a semblance of truth to those comments, they often ignore the central point to being "lucky": You need to go out and put yourself in a position to be lucky. To the best of my knowledge, no one has ever been hit by a train without being in front of it. It is the same thing with the luck. You need to get out and put yourself in situations or environments where experiences and opportunities can happen. The Greek philosopher Seneca said, "Luck is the intersection of preparation and opportunity." The main reason I put this quote in the book is to try to make myself look intelligent by quoting a Greek philosopher. But you already knew that.

Yet the essence of what Seneca said is most certainly true. Being lucky can only come about by deciding to do something and putting yourself out there. So in a sense luck can be manufactured. By preparing or getting good at something and then bringing that something into the world, you allow the possibility of serendipity to happen. If you compose amazing songs but keep them on your laptop, or are an amazing singer but only sing to yourself in the bathroom, there will be no chance for any kind of unexpected good fortune to come your way. If you want to make shit up you eventually have to put shit out there.

We opened Improv Asylum 20 years ago in Boston's North End, arguably Boston's most famous and visited neighborhood. The "Little Italy" of Boston, it is the city's oldest neighborhood and is filled with Italian restaurants, cafes, pastry shops, and more. Home to Italian immigrants in the early twentieth century, and Jewish and Irish immigrants before that, the North End is a vibrant place where locals and tourists both feel at home. With its maze of tight-laced streets and old world tenement architecture it is reminiscent of old European cities. It is well known for the Freedom Trail, Paul Revere, and heavyset men in leisure suits.

We found our theater space on Hanover Street, the main street that cuts through the heart of the North End. It was a 200-seat theater and bar below the iconic European Restaurant (Now a less than iconic CVS) and, miracle of miracles, it was empty. Seems the previous owner of the building had been stealing electricity off of the buildings behind it for the last 20 or so years, and got busted. (Yes, that element is part of the history and character of the North End as well). We could not have been more lucky; a theater and bar in the heart of the North End, surrounded by 200-plus restaurants and cafes with no other entertainment options nearby, sitting empty. We jumped at the opportunity and the rest is history.

Sooo lucky. But is that accurate? Yes and no. Yes, we were lucky to find a space in this neighborhood that was available at just the right time when we were looking. But here is the key: *We were looking!* We had decided that we wanted to grow from a small show in the basement of the Hard Rock Cafe (Clarendon Street, circa '97) to an established professional improv comedy theater (which ironically was still in a basement). From our years of doing comedy in Boston we recognized that there wasn't a professional improv comedy theater in the city. We said to ourselves, "Well, what if we create one?" So we took the next logical step to find a good location for this kind of show.

We also identified the North End as a place we should look, for all the reasons I mentioned. One of the founders, Paul D'Amato, was from the North End and knew of several places we should check out. We hit the street, opened doors, met with various property owners, and lo and behold stumbled upon a "For Rent" sign in the door of what would become the home of Improv Asylum for two decades and counting.

Lucky? You bet. On the other hand, we put ourselves out there to allow ourselves to be lucky. We took action to try to make something happen. By physically getting out into the world we exposed ourselves to far greater potential for opportunities to find us. We got out on the street and made our own luck.

The whole concept of making shit up is about doing for yourself. Making shit up is empowering yourself to try to do the things you want to do without asking permission from other people. Making shit up is about not waiting for someone else to determine your future and what you're going to do. When you become proactive and begin to do things, you set in motion a chain of events that invariably creates new opportunities, that is, luck. The more you are able to engage in new experiences, the more likely an unexpected opportunity or piece of information will make itself available to you. Like anything else, the more you put yourself into these kinds of situations, the more likely that you will recognize these opportunities.

What are some things we can do to practice getting lucky? (Yes, I am aware of all the jokes and double entendres that can be made here. In keeping with the title of this book I am choosing to keep it high-brow.) Pick something for yourself that you would like to experience a little bit of luck with. For example, you would like to have better luck fishing. Instead of going to the same fishing spot again and again and getting the same results, let's think of something new.

If I want to get lucky at fishing, is there a bait shop where I can get different opinions? What if I drive around on land or cruise around on the water looking to see where other people are fishing? What if I go to the boat shows or equipment demonstrations or lectures about fishing?

Invariably other people who love fishing will be there and I will be able to pick up information and tips that I can apply to my own quest to be a better fisherman. When I am able to finally piece enough of this information together and become more successful at fishing, my friends won't understand why I am always more lucky than they are at catching fish. The primary reason is that I put myself out there and in situations where I could learn more and get more information that I could act upon that can lead me to catch more fish.

So pick that thing you want to get luckier at. Find the different situations you can put yourself in that are remotely connected to your field of interest. If you do that enough, I guarantee luck will eventually hit you like a train.

Chapter 15

Fire the Assholes

L ife is stressful. So much to manage, so many relationships to attend
to. The last thing we need in our lives are more assholes. You know
the type; irritating, obnoxious, constantly aggravating those anywhere
near them. They have certain common traits:

They have an answer or opinion on everything, especially on things
they know nothing about.

They are great at playing "devil's advocate," shooting down other
people's ideas without offering up any of their own.

They do or say things just to piss people off.

They're always focused first and foremost on what benefits themselves.

They think that "Telling it like it is" at all times and never using tact
is an excuse for saying shitty things.

If you manage any kind of team, group, reading circle, whatever,
my recommendation to you is to "fire the assholes." They may be
high-performing, they may generate sales, they may be extremely
talented, but over the long haul the assholes will always bring a team's
performance down. Assholes are demotivational to those around
them. They create a toxic environment where people no longer want
to express ideas. While the asshole may be a top performer, the asshole
tends to inhibit the other team members from performing at a level
they are capable of.

Too often in life we allow ourselves to suffer assholes in the mis-guided belief that somewhere down the line we will reap some kind of benefit from being around these people. Assholes come in all types and sizes. They can be blustery and bullying, quiet and passive aggres-sive, seemingly friendly, or outwardly hostile. They are hot beds for gossip as well as controlling information. The asshole often holds his or herself above or away from the group. These people are excellent at pointing out why ideas probably won't work. It is the easiest thing in the world to do and any asshole can do it. I mean, come on, who amongst us can't listen to an idea and identify all the various reasons why an idea might not work? That is the entire point of calling some-thing an "idea." If it were a "thing" already, then there would be no need to have discussions around what might be possible.

There is no need to discuss if airplanes can fly if they already exist. But I'm sure back when Wilbur and Orville Wright were pitching their idea of a flying machine there was some asshole going on and on about how it would never work, and that they were stupid to try and would probably die a horrible death.

And here's the thing: the assholes are not wrong. Pointing out the obvious negative possibilities of any situation is an asshole's specialty. If they are right they get to bask in all of their "I told you so" glory. If they are wrong they shrug their shoulders and say, "Yeah, but they probably can't do it again, or keep it going, take it to the next level, make any money at it," or any number of asshole raisons du jour as to why they will eventually be right.

If you want to make shit up and do new things in your life you have to tune the assholes out. Better yet, if you can cut them out of your life altogether you will find that you will free up huge swaths of emotional and psychic energy. Looking stupid, experiencing failure, having your ideas judged are already hard enough. To then have external forces beating you down can make the act of creating damn near impossible, and at the very least extremely unpleasant.

My goal in life is to make things as easy and pleasant as possi-ble. Therefore I prune assholes with the vígor and dedication of a middle-aged suburban dad weeding dandelions from his immac-ulate front lawn. (My lawn is overrun with dandelions and I don't particularly give a shit. Pick your damn battles.)

The asshole often manifests him- or herself in the role of the afore-mentioned "devil's advocate." You know, that person in a meeting who, when an idea is offered, chimes in with:

(*Read in the most annoying tone you can possibly think of.*)
"Well, let me play devil's advocate for a second ... "

And they go on to illuminate all the ways that something won't work or the various horrible things that could possibly come from that idea. I want to jab my eyes out with a sharp #2 pencil the second I hear that person speak. Since you know how I really feel, let us look at a practical way of handling the devil's advocate in any kind setting.

Whenever I am facilitating a meeting or directing a group, a technique I use to disarm "the devil's advocate" or anyone else being overly critical during the ideation or initial creation phase is to make sure that no one can offer negative comments without having some intellectual skin in the game. What I mean by "intellectual skin in the game" is that if someone offers a negative comment or observation, I as the person in charge of the group immediately ask that person to offer an idea or potential solution on his or her own.

I will not allow someone to sit back and sharp shoot ideas without offering some of their own. When the "devil's advocate" realizes that their own ideas will be open to criticisms it is amazing how quickly they step back from the constant negative feedback of other people's ideas. In a group setting, mandating that everybody has intellectual skin in the game ensures that no one person just sits around crapping on everybody else's ideas.

There is an odd thing that I have found: the asshole tends to never leave on his or her own. They tend to just be there, day in and day out, bumming everybody out. The long-term presence of an asshole in your midst often will lead to the nonassholes leaving, which only ups the asshole's influence. When factoring in who to replace or promote, I can't tell you how much emphasis I put on whether someone is or is not an asshole. It is probably the number 1 or number 2 reason I have ever removed somebody from a position. If two people are qualified for a job, but one has more assholish tendencies, I'll always go with the lesser of two assholes.

Do not confuse an asshole with being a strong, self-confident person who speaks their mind, argues for their ideas, and isn't afraid to disagree with others. These same, nonasshole types will also argue for other people's ideas, speak up in defense of other people, and will be open to changing their mind when someone else presents a good argument or set of facts/data that create a different picture. These same people are also self-aware enough to know that they aren't always right, and willing to consider other points of view.

So if you need to make changes on your team, start with the assholes. If you are the asshole of your team, well, start that change with you.

Chapter 16

Ushers, Vomit, and Why People Clean Bathrooms

In the hierarchy of jobs at Improv Asylum the position of usher is lowest on the totem pole. It is the most entry-level position at the theater, requiring the least amount of experience and technical proficiency. People tend to start their career at Improv Asylum as an usher and eventually go into other jobs such as box office, manager, bartender, technician, and sometimes even performer. It is often a thankless job that requires a person to keep up a happy and professional demeanor in the face of oftentimes drunk blowhards who can be rude, demeaning in potentially violent.

When not dealing with these lovely people, they have to stop patrons from eating cannolis during the performance, make sure anyone who is under 21 is not sneaking booze, wake up that drunk dude in section 2, ask the bachelorette party to stop randomly screaming out the bachelorette's name during every scene, ask the couple in the back of section 4 to stop making out, immediately mop up the beer that was kicked over by the guy sitting in the front row, and stop a confused lady who is trying to go backstage because she thinks that is where the bathroom is.

Ushers are regularly accosted, demeaned, insulted, threatened, and generally treated poorly by a populace that often acts entitled and boorish. When they are not interacting with the worst of what humanity has to offer, they are mopping up piss in the bathrooms, and fishing all means of foreign objects out of the toilets, including but not limited to:

Nips of vodka
Baseball hats
Flip-flops
Gloves
Hypodermic needles
Full rolls of toilet paper
Eyeglasses
Phones
Full-sized winter jacket

On a Saturday night at Improv Asylum, they repeat these interactions and tasks over the course of four shows and 800+ guests. They do it all with smiles on their face and a great sense of humor while answering the many different questions they get from our patrons. They need to know how to talk about our training center, our private performances and corporate training programs, and all the various shows that happen at the theater.

And they have to clean up vomit. Tons and tons of vomit. Vomit in the aisles of the theater. Vomit in the bathrooms. Vomit by the bar and vomit on the stage. Vomit on the shoulder of the guy that just got vomited on, and off the lap of the woman who just vomited because her date was just vomited on. You would think these theaters were Roman vomitoriums with the amount of throwing up that is happening. Throwing up because people are drunk or sick or ate too much or are having nervous reaction to the loud noises and flashing lights. They have to clean it up fast without complaining so as to cause as little impact to the performance as possible. And they do all of this for not much more than minimum wage.

So the question is, why did they do it? It certainly ain't the money. Every usher can make minimum wage or more at some other job where they are not regularly insulted or have to clean up bodily fluids. It is not for the glory. The actors get all the applause and cheers and are constantly told how funny and talented they are. The ushers? They are mostly asked where the bathrooms are and if it is okay to change seats. So why do these smart, talented, engaging people who often have impressive day jobs submit themselves to this kind of work?

In a word, *culture*. These amazing people perform some of the most unpleasant tasks and deal with some of the shittiest people because they are part of a culture that values them for the people they are, not the position they hold. The ushers are part of a larger team whose ultimate goal is the exact same: to put on the best and funniest show possible. They are not motivated to greet our audiences with a smile or mop up the latest round of puke by net sales numbers, corporate quarterly goals, audience engagement surveys, or gross profits. They sure as shit aren't motivated by corporate sales goals and executive bonuses. They do these things because they care about each other and feel cared for by the staff and management.

The ushers show up night after night because they love the environment, the other team members, and the chance to be around comedy. Even though they have to perform some of the most menial tasks in the company, the ushers do these things because they are part of a greater ensemble. No matter what the role that someone is playing, they are valued as people. Culture is the only reason someone would stay for any length of time in a position like this.

When our culture at Improv Asylum is strong, we constantly see ushers go above and beyond what their basic duties are. When our culture is weak we see bad attitudes and high turnover in these positions. Culture is a living, breathing thing that is constantly changing. Over the course of 20 years at Improv Asylum, we have had strong cultures and weak ones. Healthy working environments and toxic ones. Teams that have worked almost magically together and others that have actively undermined each other. The commonality to a good or bad culture is leadership. Whether you like it or not, it is the leader's job to establish, maintain, and uphold a healthy culture.

As someone who has built teams and run companies for over 20 years, I can speak with authority because I have made every mistake in the book. I helped start this company because I wanted to make some funny shit up on stage and have a bar in downtown Boston. There was no plan to be in business for 20 years and grow from a regional comedy theater to a multimillion-dollar international entertainment and training company.

Just like any good improv scene, there was no real end goal – we were just following the thread and seeing where it led. Each decision we made built upon the last and, before we knew it, we had a real company. With that company came the very real challenges of managing not just a group of actors but a larger collection of people whose well-being became my responsibility.

In the early days I more or less thought that culture was a thing that just happened. My attitude was if we all just did our jobs and treated each other like reasonable human beings then the culture thing would take care of itself. If morale was low or the teams were not working as effectively as they could be, then it was the individual's fault and not the company's. I often assumed that my values and desires were the same as others, and my communication style was always understood by the recipients. In 20 years of leadership I have at times been too hard, too soft, too angry, overreactive, insensitive, indecisive, unclear, stubborn, close minded, tone deaf . . . the list can go on and on, but honestly I'm starting to make myself feel bad. The point is that I speak not as an expert who has constantly done everything right and has done nothing but win, but as someone who has made almost every mistake a leader can make at one point or another.

What I have come to understand is that the responsibility of a healthy culture is ultimately the responsibility of leadership. Those ushers are doing a fantastic job because their managers are creating an environment that they want to be a part of. Those managers are being empowered by the general managers and executives above them. The actors and members of the creative ensemble are at their best when the directors and producers are focused on building a culture where they can create in a safe and positive environment.

You may be the type of person that hears all this talk about culture and rolls their eyes. I get it. I was once that person as well. You may think that all of this is warm and fuzzy *kumbaya* bullshit. Maybe you consider yourself old-school, someone who leads by command-and-control, is hard as nails, takes no guff, and has ice water in their veins.

Good for you. You will never hear me say that teams and companies can't be led in that way. There are many ways to lead and I understand that. What I can tell you is that whether you are leading a team with a strict org chart or one with a completely decentralized decision-making process, the people on the ground actually getting the shit done on a daily basis are not doing it for any higher theory or grander cause. They are doing it for each other. They are doing it because they believe that the people right next to them care about the same things they care about. If you keep widening that circle, if the ushers believe the managers care about the same thing that the ushers do and the managers believe that the GM's and corporate office care about the same things that the managers do, you now have an extended team that feels like they are all working for each other.

While all this unabashed good feeling is great for mental health and universal karma, I am also an unrepentant capitalist. I'm in this gig for profit. As the saying goes, it's called "show business" not "show fun." A strong and healthy culture is fantastic for the bottom line.

Our ushers are the frontline for all of our different services at Improv Asylum. When our culture is strong, they are enthusiastically and authentically talking about our shows and promoting our classes. They are making our guests feel welcomed. They are making sure that the theater is not awash in vomit or being submerged in an epic fecal flood.

When I want to know how our culture is doing, I just take a look the performance of the ushers. If they are happy and having fun and not quitting in droves, then I know that the culture is strong and that managers above them are setting the right tone and leading by example.

So the next time you are at a theater or bar or restaurant or really any business that has what is often considered a lower-status position, treat those people with the utmost respect. You have no idea how hard they are working and the crazy, gross, demoralizing, humiliating things they have to deal with just to make sure that your experience is good.

And if you vomit all over the place, for the love of God, at least throw them a $20.

It will be greatly appreciated. If you want your team to reach new heights, take a good look at your culture. Because it is your culture that will propel you to the next level, no matter what level you are currently at.

Chapter 17

Diversity Is a Choice

Often when I hear people discuss how to build teams, I hear the term *diversity*. For anyone who wants to create new ideas it would seem obvious that the more diversity you have, the more creative avenues you will have to explore. Yet some people look at it and say, well, "diversity" is code for not taking the best people.

That is absolutely bullshit. To give you an example, this is the cast we put together for Improv Asylum New York: We have a gay man, a black man, a white man, a woman from Iran, and two other extremely talented women. Does this mean that because they are diverse they are somehow not the funniest people that are available? Hell, no.

They are all funny, as well as being talented writers and singers. They earned the job for those reasons, and those reasons alone. But that can't happen if leadership is not working with intent to find a diverse team. Those of us in charge have to be willing to ask, "What am I doing?" Am I not only hiring for talent and ability but for different experiences and life perspectives as well? Am I looking hard enough? Am I making sure that those people of diverse backgrounds know that they are wanted, know that they are welcome? Know that we want to see them audition? Because if we do not do that, if we just constantly bring on talent through traditional methods, we will continue to get the same results.

This is what it often looks like in my industry. You put out your audition notice, great. Everybody comes in, they audition, and you take whoever you feel are the best talent for the show you are creating.

119

Here is a fact: In the improvisational comedy business, there is a disproportionately high number of medium-sized brown-haired white guys. I am one of those medium-sized brown-haired white guys. I'm giving myself medium-sized billing, but I might be a little smaller than medium size. I know that. So if I am going to use traditional methods for casting, that is going to be what I get. That is who I'm going to see.

And there is nothing wrong with seeing medium-size white guys with brown hair. But if that is all I get to see, I am completely missing out on gigantic numbers of other talented people. So it becomes important in my role at Improv Asylum as a producer or director to make sure that if I am not getting the diverse turnout that I want, then need to make sure that other kinds of people know that they are welcome. Where should we be posting these auditions to attract diverse talent? Are we personally going out and speaking with the communities that we want to see at the auditions? Are we asking the diverse talent we are already working with where they think we should be posting audition notices to attract the talent we are looking for? Are we committed to training those diverse voices if we are not seeing them in any general talent pool?

We need to sit back and use our brains a little to consider different ways to get the results that we want. It really is not all that hard, it just takes a purposeful decision to do it.

Diversity is not a code word for, oh, well you didn't take the funniest person. That's just not true. We do take the funniest people. I also need to make sure that I am not limiting the company to only what I think is funny because as a producer, I have my own sense of humor. I do not think everything is funny, but if I am not careful, I am going to craft a show that only I think is funny, and only I will like that show. If the entire show only reflects my worldview and comedic sensibility, well sure, I am going to think it's super hilarious. Other people might be like, no, it is super lame, right?

Hey, I may love dad jokes. But maybe a whole hell of a lot of other people don't. Since I am responsible for leading an ensemble and not just creating a solo performance, I need to be very careful that the show doesn't just look or sound like one perspective. This is something we as leaders of any organization need to keep in mind. And if we do that right, if we do that in our small groups or if we do that in our larger organizations, we get access to so much more talent, so much more *funny* than you could ever think of.

When we improvise onstage, we quickly have to get on the same page, working through many, many different comedic sensibilities, worldviews, world experiences, and come together and put out a product immediately, which is hopefully hysterical comedy that makes that audience laugh. So how do we do that? Sure, we work long and hard and are funny, and have developed a comedic voice, but to survive on that stage, we have to rely on each other.

We have to support and keep each other's ideas moving forward. It isn't about only moving your own idea forward. If you only want to move your own idea forward, there is standup comedy, or one man/woman shows. Those are great venues to explore your own voice and concentrate on your own ideas. In improv we are focused on listening to the other person. I am listening to you. I am truly trying to understand the gist of what you are saying and I am now going to build off of what I heard from you, and if I know you are going to listen to me and then you are going to build off of that, then together we can fly, right?

Listening allows us to have all these different voices come together to create one show that works for an incredibly large amount of people. We cannot do a show for 200 people and have all of their same senses of humor. It would be impossible. Your sense of humor is going to be very different from mine, hers from his. But together as a group, when we go onstage, we are essentially crowdsourcing everybody else's talent and sense of humor.

So if I am a performer in a cast, sure I'm funny and talented, but man, with five other people from five different points of view from five different backgrounds, now I have access to all of that material. Now I can tap in to her funny, and his funny. I have got access to what those other performers can do, their stories and experiences. When we think of it that way, we now can crowdsource this idea of diversity to create something much more original. We have the ability to connect with and reach more people in the audience. We can create a show that is accessible to a much wider group of people

I had the opportunity to lead an improv workshop in Dubai, and it was one of the most amazing things I've ever been apart of.

These kinds of sessions are very hands on. I have people come up on stage and actually experience doing improv. Most everybody there was from the Middle East or Africa, they did not know or were not all that familiar with improvisation.

They were very buttoned up and the conference itself was called the International Association for Internal Auditors. The conference was even more boring than the title makes it sound (for all you internal auditors out there, I'm sure you are all great and super dynamic).

The coordinator of my session told me I was never, never going to get people to volunteer. And I said "I will," because I am quickly going to create a culture that will show them that it is perfectly okay for their voices to be heard. Within minutes I had, I think, 250 people up, shouting, shaking their hands and kicking their feet. People in full-on dashikis and burqas and abiyas all up doing improv, participating in all these kinds of exercises that professional improv actors do. It was absolutely amazing.

As we continued to do different improv exercises on the stage, members of the audience became more and more empowered to put themselves out there and take a chance in a way that none of them had ever done before. The different sensibilities and ideas that were presented were incredible, and though there were close to 50 different countries represented in that audience everybody was laughing because together, for just a little while, we were able to create a diverse community that accepted and supported each other.

When a team, company, or community can enthusiastically support each other, the ability to create and get shit done is exponentially increased, whereas a team, company, or community that is mired in divisiveness and negativity will always have an incredibly difficult time moving anything forward. By creating a culture where there are many voices that know they can be heard, the creative life of the team or organization has far more potential than one where it all looks and sounds the same. If your organization has looked and sounded the same for too long, look for places where you can discover new talent. Your team will be all the richer for it.

Chapter 18

Are You Worth $10 an Hour?

I was talking the other day with my favorite type of entrepreneur, a young person who has found a niche, started their own company in that niche, is hard working, street smart, and creative in operating and growing his business. So there he was in his store, I.D. Drake's Men's Consignment and Music, head down on his computer, posting and writing descriptions for sale items. Good and conscientious, right? Not so fast.

We got to chatting as we normally do and Ian began to describe the new store he is designing and planning on opening in the next few weeks. He just needs the time to finish the design work, he says. Meanwhile, he is alone in his current store posting away one laborious post at a time. So I ask him why he hasn't hired someone else to do the manual labor of uploading these images and descriptions to the website. Here is where he makes the classic new entrepreneur mistake:

Ian: *Norm, if I hire someone to do this, I'll have to pay them what, $10 an hour? So that means that those items will need to sell at a price that at least covers the cost of the person working, and quite a bit more to turn a profit. If I do the work and post the images I know that I'll at least make a profit when something sells.*
I nodded my head and continued looking around his shop. Tons of great stuff in here.

Norm: *Let me ask you something. Do you think your time and effort is worth $10 an hour?*

Ian: *Of course.*

Norm: *So you would pay yourself at least $10 an hour to work on getting your next store open?*

Ian: *Sure, I definitely would do that.*

Norm: *Then why aren't you doing that?*
    Ian looked at me in an "I'm not tracking" kind of way.

Norm: *If you agree that your time and effort is at least worth $10 an hour, then why don't you have someone else in here right now doing this work for $10 that is taking up your time and keeping you away from opening up your next store?*

It's always nice to see the lightbulb go off. Ian was making the classic cost versus time mistake that so many new business owners and entrepreneurs make. They look at a task that needs to be completed and say to themselves, "Well, it's definitely cheaper if I do it myself." And in the beginning it is. When you first start a business it is cheaper and smarter for you to do the tasks and jobs at hand. First off, you know what needs to be done (in theory). Second, you learn what is important and how to actually do the damn job. At this point you are in operator mode, and you stay in that mode up until the point where your success starts to illuminate new opportunities.

Ian was trading $10 an hour, maybe $50 over a five-hour shift, for delaying opening a store that he expects will double his monthly revenue. For 50 bucks! He admitted that he regularly spends more than that on dinner or drinks and doesn't give it a second thought. Yet here he was on a slow day at his shop doing manual labor when he could be a day closer to opening the next store that will generate much more than $50 a day.

He should have an assistant in there doing the photo uploads and caption writing. And when he pays that person $10 an hour or whatever it is, he won't be just paying that person, he will be paying himself in *time*.

Time is the most valuable thing that I have ever received from owning my own businesses. To work on my own schedule. To have the freedom to pursue what is important to me. Time to coach my kids sports or stay fit or just freaking think and listen to weird albums on my vintage grandma stereo record player.

Paying that assistant is an investment in himself. It's cheap and the ROI/ROT (return on time) is huge. As soon as you identify that there are more important tasks or ideas that you need to/want to work on in your business, hire somebody to do the things that are keeping you from doing them. To make it work psychologically for yourself (I say this because I know that oftentimes hiring someone else to do work you don't want to do is more a psychological barrier than a financial one), convince yourself that what you are paying that person is really just what you are paying yourself to do a more important job.

Go ahead, pay yourself $10 an hour. You are definitely worth it.

Chapter 19

Nobody Knows Anything

Nobody knows anything. The longer my career continues, the more I am certain of this. People think they know shit. They have ideas about things. They have thoughts and theories, hypotheses, and past studies. Yet the more things I do and the longer I do them, I have come to discover that most everybody is making shit up on the fly. And that is a good thing.

The whole point of innovation is to create something new. If we are going to create something new, then we can never be certain how it is going to work out. At some point we have to take a chance and make decisions based on the information we have at hand, our past experiences, and our gut intuition. Sprinkle in some wishful thinking and luck and we just may come up with something that nobody else has.

Much like when you figure out that "nobody gives a shit" about you, realizing that by and large nobody knows anything is quite empowering. What can be incredibly intimidating is the idea that everybody else knows much more than you do about whatever it is you want to attempt.

Clearly there are experts in every field and people who've accomplished great things and have far more experience then we will ever have at the start of something. It can cause us to have immense self-doubt in our own ability and lead us to quit before we ever even get started. I mean, everything has already been done by everyone everywhere, so what's the point? Might as well stick to the same old same old, and wait for that cold black cloud to come on down.

Don't you believe it, even for a second. There is always a way to do something new or different or better. There is always a way to compete. People like to say that for every Coke there is a Pepsi. There are also Dr Pepper, Polar Cola, Moxie, Jones Soda, Pascual Boing, Bundaberg, La Croix, Squamscot, Cheerwine, Brooklyn Soda Works, Lester's Fixin's Bacon Soda, and literally hundreds of others. There is always room for more if it is better or differentiated in some way. I'm sure at some point someone told the creators of Lester's Fixin's Bacon Soda that they were insane. Who the hell would want bacon soda, or buffalo wings soda, or ranch dressing soda? Yet they obviously believed in their own insanity and now they have a KISS-branded line of colas. They may never be Coca-Cola but that's not the point. They created something original and brought flavors and branding opportunities together in way others were not thinking about.

Even the biggest, most established brands or experts I've ever spoken with, when pressed, tend to concede that to a degree they still feel like they are making things up as they go along. I think that most of us, if we don't feel like an outright fraud, then there is a certain feeling of fooling most of the people most of the time. I mean, hey, if they are going to promote me and let me keep going then, sure, why not? Until they figure out that I'm faking it until I make it, then I will walk down the path as far as they will let me go.

The further we go down the path the more knowledge and experience we pick up, so by the time we reach a certain point we actually do end up knowing some stuff. And the best way to learn about anything is by doing it. You can study comedy all you want but until you actually get on stage and do it, it is nothing but high theory. This concept is true for just about everything; making soda, flying planes, creating an app or having sex. The true knowledge and thrill is in the doing.

Yes, I get it, you need to acquire the basic skills to pursue whatever it is that you want to pursue. In today's day and age, access to the initial information that you need about anything can be easily found. For most of human history it was the access to information that would stop or limit individuals from branching out of their small area of knowledge. If you were born into a farming family, you were most likely going to be a farmer. If you were born to a fisherman, that was most likely going to be your lot in life.

Hundreds of years ago somebody born into a fishing family who wanted to build beautiful churches most likely would never have access to even the basic information about architecture, engineering, and design. Nowadays there is open-source everything. Want to build your own rocket to go to outer space? You can find that information online. Looking to dabble in mind control or maybe the dark arts? There is a how-to guide for that. You just have to Google it. Once you start a general course of study to get the basics down, the key is to put what you are learning into tangible practice in some way, shape, or form.

Your first attempts will suck. They will. There is no getting around this. Your first rocket will blow up and your initial attempts at commanding people to do your bidding will be woefully disappointing. Everybody sucks at everything at first. That is perfectly okay. There are very few prodigies in the world, and if you are reading this book with this title, I have to assume you don't consider yourself one. I sure as hell know I am not. It makes no difference. The ability to *do* does not reside in the hands of a small minority any longer.

No longer do you have to feel that creating something is the domain of chosen virtuosos who have either been tapped by the gods or spent all of their time studying in their chosen field with the most eminent teachers available to them. If you have access to either of those things, then good for you. For the rest of us, sucking is the first step to greatness. Or at least mediocrity. Mediocrity leads to proficiency, proficiency leads to mastery, and mastery leads to excellence. It is heartening to know that the best of the best sucked at one point.

When we make shit up, the goal isn't to be instantly amazing at whatever it is we are attempting. It is to start the forward progress toward our objective. By giving ourselves permission to suck initially, we allow ourselves to create critical forward momentum. More than anything else the ability to sustain that momentum, over self-doubts and haters and setbacks, is what is needed to keep us pointed toward our end goal. Sucking and being bad at something is a temporary state. At some point you will be better equipped. At some point the state of sucking will have come to an end.

Since nobody knows anything and everybody sucks at most things, this knowledge gives us the confidence to not listen to anybody and try whatever the hell we want. Yes, of course there are plenty of people worth listening to, who have experience in whatever it is we are trying to do that is worthwhile. But even the helpful knowledge and advice that someone can impart can only be proven valid if we attempt to implement it in some way. You can get all the great advice you want, but if you are never actually willing to try, you will never know if it was truly good advice or not. Advice not acted on is mere speculation.

As a general rule I don't give advice. I am always happy to discuss my experiences and to contemplate choices and potential outcomes, but I try to avoid giving outright advice. If we adhere to the theory that nobody knows anything, including myself, then the best we can do is to try to gain an understanding of my experiences and see how these might apply to you. You, as the receiver of my experiences, then need to apply what makes sense to you and ignore that which doesn't.

If you apply what makes sense and it works, great! If you ignore the advice because it doesn't seem to make sense to you, and that works, great! The reality is that both of those situations will be true at some point. Some advice will make sense and work for you. Some advice will not make sense and not work for you at all. There will be times where you feel like you need to do exactly the opposite of what is being advised and it will work out swimmingly. There will be other times where you will ignore the advice and will fail horribly.

The commonality in all of these scenarios is that you have to decide to do something. To test the theory one way or the other. Nobody can tell you the right way to become a comedian. They can tell you of the ways things have worked or not worked out for them, but ultimately you will have to see if those same experiences and choices have the same results for you.

So go ahead and get yourself a mentor or a guru or a sage or a seer or whomever it is that can share their experiences doing the thing it is that you want to do. While their experiences are very true for them they can't really know how it will be for you. That means you have all the power to go ahead and explore whatever the hell your heart desires or your head can think of. Nobody knows anything, we all just think we do. And that more often than not that is enough to make shit happen.

Chapter 20

Who Gives a Shit?

We are all lazier then we want to be. We are all less talented, less beautiful, less rich, and less powerful. There is not one single person in my life, and I would bet $1 million in your life, who has it perfectly dialed in and firing on all cylinders. Each of us has doubts and insecurities that constantly try to pull us back from doing something more with our lives. Fear of looking stupid, of failing, of what other people will think or say cripples us in our pursuit of trying to do something just a little bit more interesting with life than we are currently doing. When all of those thoughts start dancing in your head, when the voices work themselves up into a fever pitch shouting over and over again "you aren't good enough," I want you to step back and say out loud: "*Who gives a shit?*" Seriously. Who *gives* a shit? Who gives a shit about what other people think or say? Who gives a shit if they don't think you have enough talent, or that your ideas are insane, or that you are uneducated or low class or delusional or narcissistic or any other of one million things that someone can think or say about you? Who. Gives. A. Shit.

Then I want you to answer that question and I want you to answer it out loud. The answer is simple: "*Not me!*" The sooner you can get to a place where you just don't give a shit about what others think of you, the sooner you will be in a place of confidence and freedom. Confidence to pursue whatever it is you want and the freedom to create what ever you want to create. There is so much more all of us can do if we just stop giving a shit about what everybody else thinks.

131

I mean, if all of these other people are so damn smart regarding how we live our lives, then why the hell aren't they doing better in theirs? It is because they too are making shit up as they go, and for the most part do not appreciably know any more than you or I. That doesn't mean it will stop them from offering their opinions with rock-solid certainty or be quick to offer you advice on shit they know nothing about. What it does mean is that we can care far less about other people's opinions of what we are trying to do with our lives, period.

I hold no illusions that getting to this place is as simple as snapping your fingers and shouting "Who gives a shit!?" It is a start, but only that. To find any lasting success we need tangible things that we can do or practice on a constant basis that give us the psychological and emotional strength to push through these very real mental barriers. The concepts that we explored in this book are practices that you can put into action today. With a group or by yourself, these techniques start to build up our mental muscles, which we can use to create new and interesting paths in our lives. And just like going to the gym, you will experience a certain amount of pain as you initially develop these muscles. Just like going to an actual gym, the pain fades quickly. I actually think it fades far more quickly than blasting your quads or shredding your pecks. When you allow yourself to try new things, especially things that you have always wanted to do, the rush that you get from taking those positive steps quickly begins to suppress those initial feelings of pain.

The crazy thing in all of this is that when you can truly get yourself to a place where you just don't particularly give a shit about what others think about you, the more they are drawn to you. When other people realize that you do not need their approval to believe in yourself and to take action on the things that you want to do, they tend to stop offering their opinions and start to become curious about what it is you are trying to accomplish. People tend to become far more positively engaged in what you are doing when they realize that being critical has no effect on you.

Does this mean you should be a complete dick, never listening to other people's ideas or searching out those who have more experience than you do in a certain topic? Quite the opposite. As we have already discussed, the first step in being able to make shit up is being able to listen to other people. And being a constant dick only pushes people away from you. There are already enough assholes in the world, I am certainly not advocating for more.

What I am trying to say, in a very crass and crude manner, is that we need to become comfortable with disregarding other people's opinions when they run counter to our efforts to positively attempt new things. By not giving a shit, or at least less of a shit, about what others think, we give ourselves permission to experience and achieve far more in our lives.

Some of the concepts in this book may seem like semantics. What real difference does it make if I say "Yes but" as opposed to "Yes and"? If I say no to someone's idea, am I really destroying their ability to ever come up with another one? I don't think so. And yet, it really is unbelievable the results you get when you start using these kind of positive phrases in your personal and professional relationships. Hey, maybe you are just a natural bummer of a person, always ready to see or say something negative. So here is a list of some positive words and phrases that you can start to use in your everyday dialogue:

Yes and
We should
Cool, let's
What if
We can
Agreed,
You are right
Fantastic idea
I love that
So awesome
Pretty damn good
Outstanding

People will be drawn to you simply because of the fact that people are drawn to positive energy. Positivity is hope, and hope is the thing that keeps us alive. It gets us out of bed in the morning. Hope for a better day, a better outcome. New possibilities and a greater future live in hope. If you can ignite a flicker of hope in someone else, even if it is in their subconscious, then they will be drawn closer into your orbit. The more people you are exposed to, the more ideas you will be exposed to. Somewhere in these new ideas is the spark you are looking for, to ignite your imagination and attempt something new.

Making shit up, for me, has meant many different things. It has been an art that I have practiced onstage, working with others to try to make people laugh. It has meant making this art my job, making a living building a company around the premise that if we are willing to try and fail, then we give ourselves the chance to do something far greater than we ever imagined. It has meant listening to other people and trying to understand their points of view and embrace their talents, which in turn benefits my own.

In a completely contradictory statement, making shit up has also meant not listening to other people when I felt that their views and opinions were not being offered to help me find a way forward, but rather to stop me from pursuing something far greater for myself.

We are all just making shit up as we go. If we start to embrace this concept and actually look at it as a positive, we can begin to not only embrace the crazy shit life throws at us but to actually take control of the chaos and doubts and fears that each one of us has on a daily basis.

Instead of "making shit up" being code for not knowing what we are doing, it now becomes an empowering practice where we no longer let those fears and doubts stop us from reaching for something more meaningful in our lives. The art of making shit up is simply the art of proactively living life, a life where we are more encouraging of ourselves, more forgiving. A life where we allow ourselves the chance to do something more than we or anyone else thought possible.

So get out there and make some shit up, I guarantee you will surprise yourself with what that crazy f'ing mind of yours can come up with. If you can imagine it, you can make it happen in some way, shape, or form. Best I can tell, we only get one go-around on this rock, so we might as well take our shots while we can. If we do, then at the very least we will be able to look back at some point and say we did some pretty cool shit.

Chapter 21

Everything I Know in Business I Learned from Coaching Girls Softball

IT IS POSSIBLE TO COMPETE, WIN, AND HAVE FUN AT THE SAME TIME

There are a lot of teams out there that rack up the wins, hoist the trophies, and look truly miserable. Winning and enjoying the process are not mutually exclusive. I dare say that enjoying the process makes winning, and sustained winning, more possible. Players don't want to stay on a team that they don't enjoy, no matter how many trophies you put on the mantel. Having fun doesn't mean there aren't goals and expectations. It is an attitude that says, "We expect to win and we're going to have a damn good time doing it."

YELLING MAKES THINGS HARDER

Imagine this scenario: A pop fly is hit to your second basement. It is sky-high and that 12-year-old kid is trying to settle under it without falling on their ass. Now add three coaches, 10 players, and 20 parents all yelling "Catch it! Catch it! Catch it!" That screaming is actually working against the outcome you're looking for from the player.

135

Trust me, they definitely know they are supposed to catch it. Your helpful reminder is doing f'k all to help them achieve this goal.

Sports is one of the last bastions where yelling and degrading people still passes as teaching. Instead of yelling at a player when they make a mistake, point out what they did well, for example, "Nice job of getting under that ball you, where you were supposed to be." Then give feedback that is actionable, like "Make sure you get your second hand on the ball once it's in your glove, so it doesn't pop out." Making them feel like crap when you know they already feel bad about not making the play is leadership at its worst.

PEOPLE ARE TRYING TO DO IT RIGHT MOST OF THE TIME

No kid wants a grounder to go through their legs or to overthrow first base or to strike out at the plate. In general most people are trying to do it right, whatever "it" may be. If the coach is not getting the results they want, then it is the coach's job to work with that player on the skills needed to improve the results. Shaking your head and belittling the kid in public destroys their confidence and ultimately makes it more difficult to get the results you want.

IT DOESN'T MATTER NEARLY AS MUCH AS YOU THINK IT DOES

I know, I know, the entire world will turn on the results of your U12 game against the neighboring town on a Tuesday night in mid-July. Except of course it won't. In the moment everything feels more important. The spotlight and emotions add to the pressure and can trick us into thinking that this moment is more important than it actually is. When you step back and look at the thing through a long lens it is rare that one play or decision makes all the difference in the world. If your goal is only to win that game that night, then it is easy to be swept up in the emotions of the game.

If your goal is to make the playoffs, then you may have a more measured approach to how you manage the game. If your goal is to encourage and inspire young women to compete, have fun and develop skills that will allow them to play the game long after this one particular contest, then your attitude is far, far different.

THERE IS CRYING IN SOFTBALL

There is crying in softball. Lots of it. Girls get hurt, disappointed, nervous, scared, overcome with joy, sad that they have been blocked on social media by a friend, troubles at home, school, and so on … This is true of everyone: boys, girls, men, and women. Instead of telling the kids to hide their emotions, teach them to manage how they are feeling and still be able to do what is being asked of them, even at times when their head is in a far different space. This skill is critical in a person's long-term success, whatever it is they're trying to achieve.

THE TEAM THAT MAKES THE MOST EASY PLAYS WINS

It isn't the great plays that win most games, it's the constant execution of the simple plays again and again and again. Everyone loves home run blasts or a diving catch, yet if you have to constantly rely on making great plays, you will lose more than you will win. The simple grounder to shortstop, the constant throws to first base, making contact to put the ball into play, and catching the routine fly ball are far more important over the course of the game and the season then any single fantastic play.

RELAX AND BREATHE

Take a deep breath, relax, and try to remember that while batting with two outs in the bottom of the seventh seems very different from other at-bats, in reality it is the exact same process as any of the other of hundreds of at-bats you had before.

PONIES MOTIVATE

After one particular game I was talking with one of my players and she mentioned that she had never ridden a horse before. I said, "If we win this playoff game, I'll take you and the entire team for pony rides."

This very pleasant but not overly demonstrative kid lit up. "Are you serious? You're not serious." I sure as hell was serious about it, and I told her so. Next game I had never seen her run the bases as aggressively and slide on close plays in all the years I had coached her. Talk to your players. Find out the things they get excited about and that motivate them. Yes, money will always be an important factor, yet you may be surprised what things will motivate certain individuals.

BAD COACHING RUINS EVERYTHING

And I'm not just talking about the tactics in a game. I've seen how bad coaching, mostly related to how coaches communicate with their players, take a promising young kid who loves playing the game and makes them want to quit and never pick up a glove and ball again. I've seen coaches use cutting sarcasm to belittle players, shout at kids for striking out, and tell an entire team that they should be "ashamed of themselves" for making too many errors in one inning.

No, you should never be ashamed of yourself for playing a game. The goal as a coach is to make every kid want to be on the team no matter what their role might be. I hold no illusions that all kids have the same skill sets. Here's a newsflash, neither do they. But if you can make the kid that mostly sits on the bench as excited to be a part of the team as the star player by valuing them as an individual, then you are doing your job as a coach. Don't be the coach that makes a kid quit forever. That is not how you want to be remembered.

PARENTS ARE IDIOTS

Leave your kid alone once she steps on the field. She has coaches who are telling her what to do; she doesn't need you yelling from the sidelines too. And usually what the parent is yelling is not at all what the coach wants the kid to do. Let them play the game, learn from the coaches, and find their own success.

There is nothing more annoying than a player that looks at the sideline after every swing or throw or catch. We want them to be confident in their own ability and decision making and not constantly looking for validation or criticism from their parents. The only things I allow my parents to say from the sidelines are "Good job!" and "Nice try!"

If you want to belittle your child and make them feel like crap, do it in the car ride on the way home.

GO HARD AND SLIDE

Great effort typically beats talent. Good things typically happen for the players who go hardest. Hustle, grit, and determination more often beats talent over the long haul. It is those players who start to figure out how to succeed in the face of adversity or their own shortcomings and who come to realize that working harder for your goal than those around you pays off eventually, who become the winners.

CALL IT

If it is your ball, call it. Let those around you know that this is your play and you've got it. Speak up and claim your space on the field.

YOU HAVE A JOB IF THE BALL IS HIT TO YOU, AND IF IT ISN'T

Everyone always has a job to do, even when the ball is not hit directly to you. What base are you supposed be covering? Who are you supposed to be backing up? What are you supposed to be communicating and to whom? Everybody focuses on the player with the ball but the play can't be executed if the other player isn't covering the base they are supposed to. Don't just stand around, do something.

BACK EACH OTHER UP

Stuff happens. Back each other up and limit the damage of any mistakes. A good coach applauds the kid who is constantly running in to back up a play just as much as the kid who makes the play.

POSITIVE ENCOURAGEMENT GOES A LONG WAY

Positive encouragement isn't soft or nice or touchy-feely. It is a proven and tested method of building a person's self-confidence. The goal of the coach is to get the player to believe in herself while also giving them the tools that they will need to succeed. When players see coaches giving positive encouragement it becomes contagious and the whole team starts to give that same kind of support. This amplifies the good vibes and is basically crowd-sourcing positive emotion. As the old saying goes, "If you believe you can or you can't, you are right."

YOU'RE NOT OLD SCHOOL, YOU ARE AN ANACHRONISM

"My coaches were tough and treated me like crap and I turned out okay." That's debatable. I've heard versions of this many times, this idea that, "I'm an old school coach and it's my way or the highway, dammit." Most coaches who have this attitude simply don't know how to communicate effectively what they are trying to teach. Instead they use intimidation and status to limit any kind of discourse. By limiting the discourse, they don't have to explain what it is they want. And for the love of God, you're a damned Youth Sports Coach, not some sort of latter-day Lombardi (and if you actually research coaches like Vince Lombardi or Bill Belichick, you will see that they were known as fantastic teachers).

FOCUS ON YOUR OWN TEAM

Don't worry about the other team, what they're saying, or how they are playing the game. Focus on your own team and how you can get better. Worrying about what the other team is doing or saying only serves to distract you from your real goal, which is to build the best team possible.

DON'T SHOW UP THE UMP

Yes, there are calls you don't like and that you disagree with. Showing up the ump in public gets you nowhere and usually works against you later on down the line.

IT IS OKAY TO APPEAL THE CALL

With that said, it is okay to appeal the call if you believe that it is inaccurate. Standing up for what you believe in is important. Do it in a way that doesn't make you and the people around you look like asses.

LOSING HURTS BUT DOESN'T HAVE TO DESTROY

I hate losing. I try to win each game I coach. The reality is that you will lose all sorts of games. Big games and small ones, games you are supposed to win, games you are supposed to lose. If you don't overemphasize the importance of loss and are willing to get back on the field the next day and keep grinding, you will find that you'll get your wins and begin to realize that the losses don't need to define who you are.

WINNING IS GREAT AND IS SHORT-LIVED

Winning is the best. Hooray! Ponies for everyone! Of course the last game you won has very little bearing on the next game you are playing. The only thing that really matters is how you play the next game and if you can continue to consistently put into action the good skills and habits that you have learned. Winning is the result of doing small things well again and again.

ONE OUT AT A TIME

Don't worry about getting the second out until you get the first one. Once you get the second out, then you can worry about getting the third one. Focus on the immediate task at hand and block out the next task until the first one is completed. It can be daunting to try to figure out how to get three outs against a great hitting team. Getting one out seems very manageable. Getting one out three times is simple and replicable. It keeps your team in the moment and it takes some of the pressure off of worrying about the future.

PLAY 'TIL THE END

They give you 21 outs for a reason. Play each and every one of them. The odd thing is that if you do, more often that seems likely, you find yourself with a chance to win at the end no matter how far down in the game you were. Getting your team to believe they have a chance is more than half the battle. If they believe that you believe, that's usually enough.

TAKE CHANCES

Steal some bases. Send them home from third. Pick 'em off at first. Don't just be reactive, be proactive. Try to make something happen for yourself. Don't rely on the whims of an unpredictable game. Don't be so afraid of making a mistake that you never take chances to help yourself. It builds confidence in the entire team and it's a hell of a lot more fun than just trying not to F up.

BEING IN THE DUGOUT SHOULD BE *AT LEAST* AS FUN AS PLAYING

We spend a hell of a lot of more time in the dugout than we do on the field playing the game. And not every player is going to see the same amount of time in the actual game. It is in the dugout where the esprit de corps and camaraderie is built. That is the place where everybody is equal and everybody can find the same amount of joy and pleasure, regardless of what they are doing on the field.

LISTEN TO YOUR PLAYERS

Yes, you are the head coach and you know exactly what is best for the team at all times. Never should your judgment be questioned and your authority is ironclad, never to be challenged. Also, please quit coaching right now. When you listen to your players' ideas, and even better when you can implement some of them, you get far greater buy-in from that player as an individual and the team as a whole.

You create an environment where you actually get more information because now players feel like their voices will be heard and therefore are more willing to share what they know or what they're thinking. As a coach this is an incredibly valuable. I can't tell you how many times I thought I was boosting a kid's confidence by playing them in the infield when in reality all they wanted to do was play the outfield. All that needed to happen was for that kid to feel comfortable enough to say, "Hey coach, I actually prefer playing right field." Problem solved for both of us.

By creating an environment where a player can speak up, I now have actionable information that I can use to make both the team and the player better. When the players know you are willing to listen to them it also creates less conflict when you make decisions that not everyone agrees with. More often than not, people accept your decisions as long as they feel that their voices were heard.

MAKE EACH PLAYER FEEL LIKE THEY ARE YOUR FAVORITE

The best-case scenario is that each player feels like secretly he or she is the coach's favorite. You don't do this by being fake or dishonest, you achieve this by being excited for whatever successes the player has and encouraging them when they make mistakes. When the worst player on the team and the best player on the team each feels like they are your favorite and both want to come back and play for you the next season, then you know you're doing your job incredibly well.

GET ICE CREAM AFTER A WIN

Celebrate your wins. Get ice cream and laugh and rehash the awesome plays that everybody made to help win the game. It makes life more enjoyable.

... AND AFTER A LOSS

Commiserate after your losses. Get ice cream, console each other, and eventually laugh at the plays that we screwed up. Take the sting and the importance out of our mistakes. Acknowledge that we can do better but learn how not to dwell on the past or the things we can't change that are out of our control.

GET DIRTY

Don't be afraid to dive and slide and generally get dirty. Learning to do the dirty work is a huge part of building confidence and taking ownership of your effort. When the players are celebrated for doing the dirty work just as much as for the plays that capture all the fans' attention, they learn that there are many different ways to succeed in what they are trying to do.

FOCUS ON PROCESS, NOT RESULTS

It is almost impossible to dictate the results we want. No matter how hard we try to get a hit, the ball may never get through. Getting a hit is just a result of focusing on the process of having a good at-bat. Good form, hours in the cage, hands high and tight, fast swing to the ball. Those are all the things the player can control. Focusing on the process and positively acknowledging the process even when the results aren't always what we want leads to a more relaxed approach at the plate, which then of course leads to better results.

IT IS NOT JUST ABOUT THE GAME, BUT ABOUT HOW YOU APPROACH LIFE

Almost none of our players will go on to anything greater than high school sports, and even that may be out of reach for many of them. Yet as adults we all having incredibly strong memories of our time playing on teams as a kid. We can all talk about the coaches we loved and that had a positive impact on who we are as well as coaches who made us doubt ourselves and made us want to quit.

No matter what kind of team you lead, your players will eventually move on. The goal should be to leave them with an experience that they remember fondly and give them a few tools that they can use to succeed as they move forward. Teaching people that they can achieve goals, have fun doing it, to successfully face adversity and self-doubt is what coaching is all about. The girls I have coached over the years have taught me a hell of a lot more about being a good leader, teacher, and human being than I'm sure I've ever taught them.

Remember that being allowed to coach kids is an honor and a privilege. It is easier to do more harm than good. As the coach you are there first and foremost to help the kids succeed and develop confidence that they can use for whatever they are going to do in the future.

Chapter 22

Trapped in the Bowels of the Grand Bazaar

I'm a fairly seasoned traveler. I've spent over 100,000 miles in the air to far-flung places, near-flung places and flung places in between. I feel comfortable in countries where I can't read the signs or the menus. But when I found myself deep in the bowels of the Grand Bazaar in Istanbul drinking apple tea, haggling over a beautiful Turkish rug I had no intention of buying, it was one of those moments when I fully understood that I was in over my head. But we'll get to that.

Istanbul is one of those cities that holds a magical place in the mind's eye. It is a city that has been built up and torn down many times over a couple of millenia. There are staggering pieces of history at every turn. When you go to Istanbul you are both at a literal crossroads of East and West, and a metaphysical crossroads of time and history. It is a city that I had always wanted to see, driven by my love of history as well as one of my favorite They Might Be Giants songs: "Istanbul Not Constantinople" (the "Tiny Tunes" video is a classic).

I only had a short time in Istanbul as my final destination was a gig in Munich, so I wanted to get in at least a few of the highlights: the Blue Mosque, Grand Bazaar, some good eats. Being the type of person to read up on the do's and don'ts of any particular place I'm traveling to, I did my requisite research online. I enjoy reading opinions of whether you should or shouldn't put your valuables in the safe, to carry or not carry cash, and what seems like an odd obsession of carrying that cash in a money belt fastened under your clothes like some sort of Elizabethan corset. I guess if I'm going to get mugged and have to give up my cash, I'd rather just hand it over than to also have to face the humiliation of lifting up my shirt and having said hoodlum get a look at my somewhat hairy physique. I imagine the thief taking my money and sadly shaking his head as he says in a language I can't understand:

Hoodlum: *You need more cardio and core work.*
Me: *I know! It's just that I've been traveling a lot lately and*
                        I really haven't been making time at the gym and with all
                        the buffets that are included and the hotel stays, well, the
                        stuff just sneaks up on you …

One particular warning stood out from all the rest for its detailed specificity. The helpful author had some for-real advice for any newbie paying a visit to Istanbul's Grand Bazaar:

You'll find that within minutes of entering the Grand Bazaar a friendly man will sidle up to you and strike up a casual conversation. In a short amount of time that friendly man will have gotten you to say where you are from and that he knows someone from where you are from, most likely from a specific neighborhood. In short order you'll be being lead through the labyrinths of the bazaar, deeper and deeper into the bowels of this ancient marketplace until you are deposited at a rug seller's stall where you will be served delicious apple tea and be presented hundreds and hundreds rug choices.

Well, that's a pretty damn specific scenario and one I was sure I could easily avoid. I mean it's not like some complex misdirection scam where one person is keeping your attention while another person is slyly reaching under your shirt for all that cash you have taped to your rib cage like some sort of mule for a Columbian drug cartel. (I have been binging *Narcos* on Netflix. No offense meant to Columbia or any of the cartels.) This seemed to be a pretty obvious situation that could be avoided.

So there I am with my travel companion at the majestic Grand Bazaar, the ancient marketplace where traders, travelers, and merchants have bartered and haggled and tried to get the better of each other for eons. Me, I was just looking to stroll through the corridors and kiosks, taking in the sights, sounds, and smells of this very old mall. My travel partner, well, he collects snow globes. Hey, to each their own. So he steps into a vendor's stall that sells snow globes. Yes, apparently that's a thing you can get at the Grand Bazaar in Istanbul. As I stood outside waiting for my companion to purchase an authentic Turkish snow globe, sure enough a friendly gentleman approaches me and begins chatting me up. Being a Bostonian I am very adept at the "no thanks, not interested, leave me alone" vibe. You could try to hand me a hundred-dollar bill and I would be mumbling, "I'm all set, I'm all set, no, thank you, I'm all set."

So I was feeling fairly confident as the gentleman casually asked where I was from. Now, asking where someone is from is one of those questions that tends to reach down into one's brain in such a way that it is almost impossible not to answer. I've gotten quite a bit of advice from people on how to answer this question in a foreign country. By and large, the answer most generally suggested is, "Say you're from Canada."

Apparently saying "I'm from Canada" is the universal phrase for "I am incredibly nice and of no threat to you and you will get nothing of interest from me." I did not use the "Canada" defense but instead uttered the words "I'm from Boston." What an asshole I am. As my travel companion took an interminable amount of time choosing between the snow globe with the Blue Mosque in the center and the one with the little boats on the Bosphorus, my new found friend became excited at the mention of Boston and let me know that he too used to live in Boston. Brookline, in fact. Well, no kidding? I spent the better part of my 20s living in Brookline and Brighton on the edges of Boston. My new friend, Sam, definitely his real name, proceeded to pull out his iPhone and show me some pictures of his friends who are still there.

While all this was going on, what I consider to be one of the most amazing demonstrations of subtle psychological influencing happened. I found myself walking with Sam deeper and deeper into the bowels of the Grand Bazaar where I was deposited at a rug seller's stall and handed a delicious cup of hot apple tea. Clearly my mind is so fragile that I can be influenced far, far more easily that I have ever imagined. I now know that if I am ever in a situation where I am being interrogated, a bit of friendly conversation and something tasty will be all it takes for me to spill any and all trade and state secrets.

As I was shown various different rugs – Persian, Turkish, Indian, nothing that looked like it would be offered for 70 percent off on Wayfair – I started to regain my wits and realized that I did not know where I actually was or how I had gotten there. Nor did my traveling companion. As I continued to listen to the merits of the various rugs being proffered I started to explain that, no, I wasn't interested in the shipping prices to the USA and that no, I wasn't in the market for a carpet at all.

Sam, by now my very good friend who I was definitely going to meet up with the next time he was in Boston, which was very soon, he assured me, inquired as to whether my travel partner might be interested in a rug. Me, saying the only thing a true and stalwart friend would say when it looks like another might be drawn into a wicked web of deceit and commerce, immediately said, "Yes, I think he might be."

Sam ducked out of the stall and the hard sell stopped as I was offered more tea and some sort of delicious pastry with candied nuts on top. Within minutes my companion stumbled into the stall somewhat confused as to just what was happening. The rug merchant handed him some hot spiced apple tea and said, "Your friend mentioned you are interested in purchasing some of our fine carpets." I just shrugged my shoulders and gave him a half-assed look that said, "Sorry dude, I had to say *something*."

Forty-five minutes later we were exiting the bazaar and my friend was holding receipts for a lovely Turkish area rug and a lush, Persian throw along with his snow globes (he bought both). I was on an airplane to Munich less than 24 hours later. I'll be back, Istanbul, and your apple tea and candied nut cakes won't win me over so easily next time (they definitely will).

Chapter 23

The Ambassador
and the Bathroom

I have a finely tuned bathroom radar. I can sense a bathroom within 360 degrees of my location a hundred yards out. This skill has evolved over many years of finding myself in bodily function emergency situations. These scenarios are typically self-induced, mostly driven by my obsession with spicy food and love of street meats. The sweat beading on my forehead and a general feeling in my entire body of the sudden need to evacuate whatever has been recently put inside it is a common experience. I live in a constant state of low-level dysentery.

Speaking of low-level dysentery, I found myself in Washington, DC. I was here for a meeting with an NGO followed by an invitation to the Irish Embassy for an event in the evening. In 20 years in the entertainment, comedy, and improv training world, I have been pitched all kinds of strange concepts. A Russian billionaire wanted my company to supply actors dressed as bunnies playing improv games at their wedding (I passed on that one, and in hindsight, I definitely should have taken this gig. The stories would have lasted for years). I have done improv with Special Forces soldiers, conducted role plays where we acted as douchebag managers at Harvard Business School, and have written bad jokes for robots. I've done some weird stuff. When I was contacted by an international NGO and asked if I would be interested in meeting to discuss how our improv techniques might be employed in negotiations with African warlords, I mean, how could I possibly say no?

The skill set of improvisation, at its core, is the ability to listen to other people and build off of their ideas with the goal of getting to a place or idea that both parties have agreed to and feel ownership of. Apparently negotiating with warlords requires much of the same skill set, namely, trying to move the conversation in a positive direction and working toward a resolve that all parties can agree with. One major difference is that if the conversation doesn't go well you may be killed.

Dying on stage is an occupational hazard, albeit a metaphorical one. And while it most certainly does not feel good, you still have the ability to go to the bar afterward and commiserate with your cast mates. That opportunity does not typically exist on the Warlord Circuit.

The meeting itself was fantastic and it really was fascinating to discuss the similarities that exist in the techniques that high-level negotiators use and the skill set that professional improv comedians employ to manage stressful situations. The ability to focus on another person and read the room is a skill used by both improv comedians and high-level negotiators. Moving through a conversation without a script requires a deft touch where one places their own wants in the background, for at least a little while, as they ride the flow of information to wherever it may take them.

Our hosts had invited us to an event at the Irish Embassy later that evening. I was very excited to have the opportunity to hob elbows and rub nobs with the movers and shakers of the international do-gooder set. It's always fun to respond to the question of "And what is it you do?" posed by someone who has recently rebuilt a village or brought healthy water to a region or peace to an ancient tribal conflict, by saying "I make shit up for a living."

With dreams of Bond/Bourne/Ripley dancing in my head, our team made our way to the Embassy. Nearing the end of our Uber ride was the moment when that old familiar feeling started to spread through my body. The beads of sweat, the glassy-eyed stare, the suddenly becoming quiet as I focused my mind on controlling the internal workings of my systems. I was now what I refer to as being "on the clock" and so my bathroom radar powered itself up and was working in overdrive.

We pulled up to the stately Irish Embassy where all the lovely people in tasteful suits and dresses were making their way into the facility. Upon entering the building a reception line snaked up the sweeping staircase where an elegant woman was laughing and greeting the guests. Scanning the immediate vicinity, my radar told me that what I needed was upstairs, past this woman who was holding up the damn line with her charm and good humor.

Using my best mental mojo and the well-honed technique of not squeezing too tightly or too loosely, I moved up the spiral staircase one agonizing step at a time. While all around me was the buzz and excitement of well-intentioned people about to get free meat on a stick and complementary booze, I heard nothing but the swooshing of my stomach. As I finally reached the top of the stair I came face-to-face with the hostess. She extended her elegant hand and said " Thank you so much for coming. What is your name?" I offered my clammy palm, and looking over her shoulder, trying to identify which of the doorways was the one that I needed, replied, "Norm Laviolette, and you would be?"

There was a moment of slight confusion in her face, then she replied, "I would be the Ambassador." My instinct in these kinds of situations has always been to double down on the faux pas, if for no other reason than the fact that humor has more often than not gotten me out of whatever predicament I have gotten myself into. With a smile and a firm handshake I declared, "Then you must know where the bathrooms are." She pointed down the hall and to the left, at which point I excused myself and nearly ran to my final destination.

The rest of the evening was a heady mix of international glamour and high-level conversations on how to make the world a safer and better place. I focused on the scallops wrapped in bacon and getting drinks from the different bars so as to not look like a complete drunk by getting too many from the same bartender.

I never was asked to make the trip to Africa and sit with warlords, which is unfortunate. I was very much looking forward to the opportunity to see if my wits and charm, which to this point has allowed me not only to stay alive but to thrive, could be employed to end some conflict or another.

I have the scenario perfectly pictured in my head. I enter, along with our small team of negotiators into the home of some powerful warlord.

The tension is thick and the silence is heavy. Their side eyes us with suspicion as we try to hide the anxiety and fear we are feeling. When it seems that the tension can't climb any higher, I clear my throat and look the warlord right in the eyes and say, "Hey, you must know where the bathroom is around this joint, right?"

Chapter 24

China Talk

I am very fortunate to travel around the world working with groups and giving talks about improv comedy and my experiences in creating not only shows but companies dedicated to the art of making shit up. Recently I had the amazing experience of working in Shanghai and Beijing. The following is a transcript of a talk and the Q and A session that I gave deep in the old city section of Beijing.

I want to tell you a little bit about who I am and my background. I'm Norm Laviolette. I'm a co-owner and cofounder of a place called Improv Asylum in Boston. We founded the company in 1998. So we're on our 20th year, and I've been doing comedy for 20, 23, 25 years, something like that.

I'm very fortunate. I'm doing what I love to do. It's my day job, it's my night job. It pays the mortgage and provides for the kids and the wife. And yet for me, the basic premise of all that hasn't changed, which is why I started doing this way the hell back when I was far younger than all of the people in this room. And for me, what matters is the love of the work.

What I mean by the love of the work is that the stuff that you're doing to get better is really the thing. Of course we love the shows. That is why we do what we do. We love to play the game, right? We love the shows. Who wouldn't love doing the shows and have people tell you you're funny, but, oddly enough, that will not sustain you. Because probably for most of you, you're not doing shows five nights a week.

So to get to where you want to go – we talk about professionalism, right? And what that means. Professionalism isn't just what you do on the stage. That's actually probably the smallest amount of what you're required to do. The professionalism is applying that same commitment to when you get amped up and you are ready and you're committed to do the work in your shows, and it's the same as your rehearsals, or in the other parts of what you're trying to do with your career, be it searching out and finding a venue, or trying to find an agent or a manager.

If you want to be professional, you have to treat it like your job, even when it is not your job. Right? And so for me, when I got started in comedy, I started at college. And I decided that for whatever reasons I was funny and I was going to start doing comedy.

I'm not saying I was funny, 'cause I wasn't. I just didn't know that. And it's kind of irrelevant whether you are or you're not, as long as you think you are, that's good enough. And so I started in college and I created a really shitty college TV show. It was called *Beyond the Norm*, but I loved it. It was really fun. I love puns. That's my Instagram thing, too: Beyond the Norm And.

I loved doing it. It was so fun. I had a great time. The quality didn't matter necessarily in the starting of it, but I had the drive to do it, to keep making it happen, and what I found very early on is that there's really nobody that's going to essentially help you make it happen.

Nobody owes your brilliance and talent anything. They don't really need it, and if you think about it, that's actually very liberating. Because if you accept that as a truth, it kicks you in the ass and you realize that you got to go do it yourself, and then oddly enough, when you start doing things yourself, people start to find you.

So as I started doing comedy in college, I applied that same thing to my career as I moved out of school and I started doing this in the city. I did improv. I did stand-up, any kind of comedy where anybody was willing to let me. And I think that's how I started.

That's why I never developed a real adherence to any one hard-core improv philosophy. And even then when I started, when I started doing comedy, I was living in a five-bedroom apartment in Boston.

My room was a pantry. I kid you not, it was. I could touch the walls with my hands. I hung my clothes in a closet in the kitchen.

But I was doing comedy in the city. Not particularly well and not often, but I remember thinking to myself, clearly to this day, I can remember being in that room watching TV and I remember thinking to myself, I've made it. I was like, I got my own room in a big city, I'm doing comedy, like this is it, right? And even then, even when really nobody wanted me and nobody was paying me, I had decided and identified for myself that this is what I do and I decided for myself that I was a professional and that dictated and drove all my decisions going forward.

I treated it like my job even when it wasn't my job. And what that does is that I started to develop certain habits and ways of committing to what I wanted to do in comedy and in my career and it informed the steps I would take. Well, if this is my job, if I don't want to do anything else at some point in my life, then I really better treat this not as a hobby but like what it is I want to do.

Now I'm not saying there's anything wrong with doing this as a hobby. It's irrelevant. I've seen people who do this work as a hobby that are the most brilliant people in the world. That isn't a measure of whether you are good or not good. It's just for me from a professional standpoint, this is what I wanted to do. So, that's what I did. And by doing that, treating it that way, every step of the way, I started doing more shows and met more people and then the opportunities came. Then it was time to say, well, what is the next level to make it more professional?

And so for us, we formed a troupe and we did regular shows at the basement of the Hard Rock Cafe in Boston. And then what was the next step out of that, to be more professional and do more? That was to get our own venue, right? That was the next step, so we went out and we searched and we found our own venue, but each decision to answer the question "How can I be more professional" led me to the next level of how to be more professional.

We found a 200-seat theater and bar in the heart of Boston's North End, which is the oldest part of the city. At the time I was 26 years old with my two partners and we decided, we'll try to get that lease. We had to sign on to a commitment to half a million dollars over five years.

So there is the point in your scene where you have to make a decision, right? What do you want to do? Do you want to try to do this and be professional or do you want to say, I'm going to walk away. I'm not going to take the risk. It's gonna be different for everybody, okay, but for me it was a question of what we talked about. One issue is that I was 26 at the time. Right? So we had said that at age 40 I would want to know if it worked, or I would want to know if it didn't work. But I don't want to be 40 wondering what would have been.

So we made the decision, we went and, and look, it's worked out so far and I'm just past 40. No, I'm not just past 40, and so that's the final thing I would leave for you. I really want more question and answer in the sense of, well, if you want to do this right, how do you treat it like your job when it's not your job, and how do you keep making those decisions that lead you to the place that you want to go, but you keep making those decisions and you will then come up to a point where you are like, oh shit, they will let me do this, and here's the cost of entry.

Then you make your decision and you live with it from there. So that just gives you my background. So now I want to hear from you. Do you have any questions about what I do, about what you want to do, anything like that?

Q: *So one point we emphasized is details today, right? Like little things. Is it true that the longer we work together, the longer the team is practicing, the more we're able to notice these details?*

A: *Yes, that is true. You're talking about two different things. So the longer the group works together, the more in tune the group will be with each other. The attention to detail will be a more individual thing to start. You don't need a group mind to name the damn title of the book in your scene. Well, what will happen is if you start to pay more attention to detail and you named the damn title of the book, the people around you will start to be like, hey, they all laughed when he named the damn title of the book. I should do that more. So you have, even though it's a group mind, you have individual responsibilities.*

Second question?

Q: *People's level of improv is different and maybe some people even if you keep telling them a thousand times, they still don't listen. They don't have those skill sets. A term that he uses is the maturity of the mind, like self-awareness is one of those things. How do you deal with that?*

A: *Do you want the improvisational politically correct answer or do you want my answer?*
(Crowd laughs and calls out "Both!")
The politically correct improvisational answer is to continue to support them and give them tools and techniques to get them to a place where they can better execute what it is you're asking them to do. Would you like my answer? If they're not able to get it down after a certain amount of time, you probably need to move on from them, but that's the professional answer, right? If your goal as a community, a support center, or an improvisational collective is to keep everybody in at all different skill levels, well, then of course the first answer is the correct answer for that organization. The professional version of this is, this ain't a club, it's up or out at some point, you know, because you got to get better.

Other questions?

Q: *So how does a group get better when they're all at kind of a similar level and they don't have like a coach on the side or someone to help them along. How do they collectively get better?*

A: *Get a coach! (Laughter!) I don't mean to be a jerk about it, but like find somebody that you think is even marginally better than you. Maybe somebody who's been doing it like six months longer than you and say, hey, can you coach us? Can you put some things together? Because even that, just having that outside eye just a little bit, who maybe knows like two more exercises than you, can see more from the outside looking in. I look around this room and I look on the stage and I see plenty of people that would be fine for coaches.*

Next question?

Q: *How do you practice without a coach? Just by yourself or as a group, are you just going to go down the wrong path by yourself?*

A: *I think if you practice by yourself, you'll plateau at some point. Like, it's a great way to start, but you will plateau because you won't have anybody calling you out on your bullshit. You're going to all be nice to each other and it'll be like, that's really great. And then you're going to go to the bar and we're going to be like, fucking Jesse, man, Jesse. And you're going to do that at the bar and it—*(calling out to Jesse in the crowd) *Sorry Jesse, I thought you did a great job!—and so at some point, if you want to progress past the "this is just fun and I'm working on my brain and we're having a good time," you will need to get somebody that can kind of hold you to a plan.*

Another question?

Q: *Do you have any plans to produce any books for the Chinese market? There are very few resources about improv in Chinese that have been translated. One of the few being* Truth in Comedy *by Charna Halpern. Uh, that's one that's like the bible that everyone has read, but there's not a lot of books out there.*

A: *Are you a publisher? Because I'm open to a deal! Oh, you know, everywhere we go, Bob, I get the "write a book" thing. I got to get off my ass and write the book. I do, I do. It is something that I think is in the future for us, but, but there are, there are books out there. Look, Charna's book is great for starters. I really like Mick Napier's book* Improvise. *UCB certainly in the past couple of years, put out a tome and that's pretty good. I mean it's pretty in-depth. The caveat that I put on it is that UCB is one way to think about improv. It's not the only way to think about it. But functionally, that's one of the best books out there. And then also recently some good friends of ours from Texas put out a book called* Happy Accidents. *It's a group called Four Day Weekend. They are very good friends of ours and it's a fantastic book.*

Okay, great. So I know we had another question over here.

Q: *Is there anything we can do in everyday life to practice improv skills?*

A: *Absolutely. The core of improvisation is fully listening to other people. You can practice that at every moment of every day when you are interacting with people. But make a game of it, right? To make a game of it, what I used to do and I sometimes still do when I'm in horribly boring meetings is I will try to play back their sentence exactly as they said it. Every sentence in my mind, sentence by sentence, to practice getting the entire line of dialogue down. This does a couple of things. First, it makes me not want to kill myself during the meeting. And second, it works on that muscle of listening to the entire line of dialogue and understanding it and being able to replay it. So I think that's like the easiest thing to do or most readily accessible. If you're alone, why don't you go do stand-up or tell stories? I mean that very seriously. I really, really do. I get it. I come from Improv, but it's super culty, you know? Trust me, I know, I help it, I profit from it, I get it. But honestly, I think sometimes we focus way too much on improv. You know how you can get better at improv, go understand the mechanics of stand-up comedy even if you're never going to use them. Find storytelling opportunities. In the states, there's a thing called the Moth. You have the Moth here? Great, that's the thing I tell every improviser do, is go do the Moth, go tell stories, learn to be on stage by yourself 'cause that'll inform your improvisational work later on.*

So five minutes for more questions.

Q: *So there's a lot of different schools of improv in the states. How is Improv Asylum different, what is your style? What's the level of Improv Asylum? So they want to look for the right trainers to come and they don't really know what kind of criteria they should be looking at. So this is a chance to sell IA!*

A: *Sure, It's the absolute best and everybody else sucks. No, no, no, I'm kidding! So our style, our style is kind of what I said earlier.*

We focus on scene work and relationships. That's the main thing. There's other schools of thought that will focus on game or character. Our primary focus is on relationship within the scene work and then of course you will find game. You will find character within that. So that's number one in terms of what we focus on. The second thing that we do from a performance standpoint is we love talking and interacting with the audience. We just love it. So from a performance standpoint, we really, really emphasize that within our own shows. We do it not because it's dogma, it's because that's just what we like to do. Right? So, when we train and much like what you just saw, we will focus on really good relationship and scene work because we, and I firmly believe that if you have that, you can then apply it to however it is that you want to do it, be it improvisation, be it long form, be it short form, be it sketch, or be it the written word.

Certainly we like to take suggestions from the audience to drive a lot of our work, but more so now our shows are like conversations. We love to just talk. We love to say, what do you do? What's your story? And we love to get into this conversation and people share so much crazy shit that you'd be shocked. People will start just emptying their soul to you in front of like 200 people and you can see in their eyes they are like, I don't know why I'm saying all this! What it does though is it certainly gives us rich material to mine on stage, but the exchange of the information really kind of brings the audience together, and we really enjoy that. The audience wants to participate, I don't see why you don't let them.

I know we're coming up on the end. Any last questions?

Q: *What's your best audience warm-up to get them relaxed and ready for the show?*

A: *So we keep things real simple. Right, so our audience warm-up is real quick and easy. We don't like to get too elaborate and too fucking crazy with all this. So honestly speaking, this is what a show looks like for us to warm up an audience:*
"Awesome. Give yourselves a round of applause. I'm psyched you guys are here. This is great. Hey, look, we want to warm you

up real quick and ask you some simple questions. I'd like you to respond as a group. Can you do that? "Yes." Excellent, So what's your first name? That was terrible. Yeah, cut that shit out. What's your first name? Where did you grow up? Who was your best friend in middle school? Who was the first person to ever break your heart? Shit just got real everybody! You think we're just gonna make laughs and stuff. No, we're going to dig down deep. We're going to make you cry. All right, you ready to go, you ready for a show?"

There it is, that's the warm-up. Okay. And the point is, the point is let's keep it simple. The audience is already going like, especially in a newer market like this, the audience is already saying "What is this? What's going on?" It's all individual or group aesthetic. The IA style isn't to nerd and geek out the audience, it just isn't. So that's kind of how we do it.

So I know that we're out of time. I'm going to be hanging around if anybody wants to chat individually. I will say this. It was true last night and it is true tonight. You folks are fantastic, and not only are you fantastic, but you have an opportunity to manifestly change the dynamic of how your culture or a culture of a country works together and creates. And while you may feel like you don't have a lot of resources at your disposal, you don't need them. And that is a really, really huge advantage and bright future that you have. Just go make shit up and blaze your own path and people will follow.

AUTHOR'S NOTE ON "SHIT"

If you have read all the way to the end of this book, most likely you have either become immune to or annoyed by the constant and gratuitous use of the word "shit." Sure, I've thrown in a few "assholes" for good measure, but mainly focused on the catch-all curse word "shit."

There are several reasons why I decided to use the word so liberally in this book. First off, whenever anyone asks me what I do for work I always answer flippantly, "I make shit up for a living." It is intended as a humorous response to a general question and hopefully conveys that while I may take my work seriously, I do not take myself nearly so. Second, I am using it for affect. When I teach or direct improv, one of the things that often comes up is swearing. Should you or shouldn't you? Is it cheap or easy? Does it alienate an audience or bring them closer to you? The answer, of course, is in your own personal preference and also the audience to which you're performing for. You can be just as funny on stage working "clean" as you can working "blue" or "dirty."

You do need to be cognizant of your audience. If you were doing an afternoon matinee show for families, one would rightly make the decision that we should be avoiding swears so as to make the audience comfortable and allow them to enjoy the performance. If you attend the midnight show on Saturdays at Improv Asylum called "Raunch," then you can expect to see some really nasty shit, and if you didn't, you would most likely be very disappointed.

Whether you swear a lot or a little or not at all onstage, what we want actors to understand is that curse words are the verbal equivalent of the crash of a cymbal. It tends to be jarring and typically accents, in a loud way, other ideas. Used correctly swears can drive home points and ideas in a memorable way. Used constantly, they can drown out all of the other good stuff that is being said. It is hard to listen to a song that is accompanied by mostly cymbals.

I also wanted to attempt to write a book that sounds, at least to a degree, like the world I grew up in and the world in which I worked. There are many other books of similar subject matter that use lovely and gentle flowering language that is pleasing to the ear and goes to great lengths to offer no offense. That is not this book. There are exactly 108 times the word "Shit" is used in this book.

Did I use the word shit too much? You will have to be the judge of that. Ultimately, I decided to take a tone that was both true to myself as well as different from other improv/business books. I did this even against the advice of some smart and talented people. This decision is yet another example of how sometimes, hell, oftentimes, you just have to do what you think works best for you.

I can't thank you enough for reading this book and hopefully our paths will cross at some point, be it in real life at one of the talks or seminars that I do around the world, or at one of my theaters or clubs, or online. I am always happy to talk about things related to improv and comedy in the business thereof. If I have offended anybody with the relentless use of the word "shit" or any of the other curse words that have appeared on these pages I would just like to say: I don't give a shit.

N

ETYMOLOGY OF THE WORD "SHIT"

The word shit entered the modern English language via having been derived from the Old English nouns *scite* and the Middle Low German *schite*, both meaning "dung," and the Old English noun *scitte*, meaning "diarrhea." Our most treasured cuss word has been with us a long time, showing up in written works both as a noun and as a verb as far back as the fourteenth century.

Scite can trace its roots back to the proto-Germanic root *skit-*, which brought us the German *scheisse*, Dutch *schijten*, Swedish *skita*, and Danish *skide*. Skit** comes from the Indo-European root *skheid-* for "split, divide, separate," thus *shit* is distantly related to *schism* and *schist*.***

**Oftentimes an improv or comedy scene is referred to as a "skit." Oh, the irony.

***Snopes.com

ACKNOWLEDGMENTS

The number of people who have impacted my life over the past 40 years is truly stunning when I look back to consider where I came from and where I am now. First and foremost, I would like to thank all of the incredible people that I have had the privilege to work with over the past 20 years at Improv Asylum and Laugh Boston. From actors and comedians to co-owners, from front of house to corporate office, to music, tech, students, and audiences, each individual has left an indelible mark on who I am today. Nothing I have achieved happens without all of you. "Thank you" does not even begin to convey the gratitude that I have toward all of you, but it is a start.

It is a rare thing when people in your life support you to the point where success or failure almost does not seem to matter. My incredible wife Kelly decided it was a good idea to date a comedian who lived in a pantry, and has stuck around ever since. So much of what I have achieved comes directly from the fact that this amazing woman never once questioned what I was doing or why. That kind of faith breeds incredible confidence. Or madness. Either way, this doesn't happen without her.

To my oldest friends from Grafton, Massachusetts: We may have shared our formative years together, and in this we are not so unique. The fact that you so vocally and personally continue to support all the crazy shit that I do makes me incredibly proud to still say I'm a kid Straight Outta Grafton.

To the UMass gang: It was you who first made me believe that comedy might be a thing I could do. From the TV show *Beyond the Norm*, to *Mission Improvable*, to the huge tips you would give me for all the free food I gave you at the Top of the Campus, knowing I would give it all back at Time Out, you have always been there to laugh when I wasn't funny, to buy my beers when I couldn't afford them, and believe in me when I had my doubts.

165

Like many things in my business and career, this book doesn't get done without all of the efforts of Bob Melley. The proverbial bull in a china shop, he is the epitome of the person who gets shit done. Thank you for helping me get so much shit done.

To my sisters Lori and Karen, who always treated their baby brother like he was something special. He wasn't, but because of you, he sure felt like he was.

Last, to my parents, the late Cécile Grégoire and Norman "Big Norm" Laviolette Sr. There never was or will be any bigger fans of who I am and what I do than them. These two, an auto-factory worker and a truck driver, supported and encouraged me to pursue what must have seemed like completely foreign and frankly insane goals, with never a trace of cynicism or bitterness. They rooted the loudest and longest at every step of the way, and made me believe, probably unrealistically, that I could do any damn thing I wanted. No one would have been prouder than them of this book, and my only regret is that they are not here to annoyingly brag to everyone they know that their "Little Norm" is a big-shot comedian and author. They liked to lay it on thick, and I loved every minute of it.

ABOUT THE AUTHOR

Norm Laviolette is it a comedian, speaker, writer, business owner, entrepreneur, and girls softball coach. Norm grew up in Grafton, Massachusetts, and attended the University of Massachusetts at Amherst, where he is still a few credits shy of graduating, thanks to that damned French class. He is a former member of the Massachusetts and Vermont Army National Guard. Norm cofounded the acclaimed improv and sketch comedy theater Improv Asylum, with locations in Boston and New York City. Norm speaks around the world about how the philosophies of improv can be used to transform teams into more powerful, creative, and healthy organizations. He lives with his wife, two daughters, two dogs, and a cat named Kenny in Duxbury, Massachusetts.

INDEX